How to

Communicate

from the

Heart

Transcendence Toolbooks, vol 3

How to

Communicate

from the

Heart

KIM MICHAELS

MORE TO LIFE PUBLISHING

www.morepublish.com

For foreign and translation rights,

contact info@ morepublish.com

ISBN: 978-9949-518-39-5

Series ISBN: 978-9949-518-04-3

The information and insights in this book should not be considered as a form of therapy, advice, direction, diagnosis, and/or treatment of any kind. This information is not a substitute for medical, psychological, or other professional advice, counseling and care. All matters pertaining to your individual health should be supervised by a physician or appropriate health-care practitioner. No guarantee is made by the author or the publisher that the practices described in this book will yield successful results for anyone at any time. They are presented for informational purposes only, as the practice and proof rests with the individual.

For more information:

www.ascendedmasterlight.com

www.transcendencetoolbox.com

CONTENTS

INTRODUCTION

The idea behind *Transcendence Toolbooks* is to give you effective tools for shifting your consciousness. Many spiritual books give you understanding, and while this may be inspiring, it does not necessarily lead to practical change. This book contains a unique combination of teachings and techniques for invoking spiritual light. Both the teachings and the invocations are given by the universal spiritual teachers of humankind, also known as the ascended masters. The combination of teachings and exercises has the potential to help you go through a real transformation that will bring you to a higher level of your personal path.

This book is designed to help you unlock your potential for communicating in a way that is distinctly different from what we normally call communication. You have the potential to communicate by letting the energy and the wisdom of your higher self flow through you. Doing this will help you breach the gap we often feel when trying to communicate with other people. It will help you break free of the patterns that so often block communication and mutual understanding. Learning to communicate from the heart can open up for the fulfillment of your life's higher purpose, your personal divine plan. This will give you a unique sense of accomplishment and meaning. The teachings and tools in this book are given by representatives for each of the seven spiritual rays. If you are not familiar with the ascended masters and their teachings, it is recommended that you read the book *The Power of Self,* which explains who the masters are, how they can help you and how you can follow the path to self-mastery offered by the masters. You can also find information on the website: *www.ascendedmasterlight.com.*

The invocations following each chapter are meant to be read aloud by you. You can read them in a slow, meditative way or you can give them faster and with more power in your voice. There is no one right way to give the invocations, but they obviously cannot work unless you read them aloud. If you desire more detailed instructions for how to give invocations, please visit the website: *www.transcendencetoolbox.com.* You might also find it helpful to give the invocations along with a recording. You can purchase and download sound files of the invocations from the website: *www.morepublish.com.*

It is suggested that you start using this book by reading the first chapter and then giving the first invocation at least once, perhaps several times. You can then move on to the second chapter and so on until you have worked through all seven chapters and invocations. Once you are familiar with the teachings, you do not have to read the chapter before giving an invocation, yet you will probably find that reading at least part of a chapter helps you get more out of giving the invocation.

There is no right or wrong way to use the invocations. As one example, you might give one invocation per day until you have given all seven and then start over. You might do this four times, which takes almost a month, and this will give you a good feel for the power of this ritual. You can, of course, continue this daily ritual for as long as you like. Another powerful approach is to give the first invocation once a day for nine days, then give the second for nine days and so on. It is recommended that you use your intuition to sense how you can best adapt the tools to your personal situation. You might be prompted from within to give one particular invocation every day until you feel you have gained the result you need at this time.

Depending on your speed, it takes 15-25 minutes to give one invocation. This means you can give all seven invocations (one after the other) in around two hours, which is a very powerful ritual. If you decide to do this, you do not have to give the opening prayer or the sealing with each invocation. You give an opening prayer when you start and the sealing after you finish the last invocation.

Feel free to be creative in the use of the tools included in this book. For example, you can give the matrix for another person or persons with whom you desire a higher form of communication, even for the healing of the collective consciousness.

If you make the effort to overcome your initial resistance and build a momentum on giving the invocations, you will likely find that it is one of the most powerful and effective spiritual tools you have ever used. By combining this tool with a willingness to look into your own psyche and let go of limiting beliefs, you can turn your life into an upward spiral that will expand your ability to communicate. Truly, as the masters say, everything revolves around your free will. If you can accept that transcendence is possible for you, then the results will be manifest for you. Invoke, and ye shall receive.

Because this book contains teachings and tools from the seven spiritual rays, the first chapter will give a brief introduction to the rays, their qualities and the ascended masters who embody those qualities. The following chapters will then give the teachings from the masters of the rays.

1 | INTRODUCING THE SEVEN RAYS

Who created the material universe, including planet earth? It was done by a number of beings called the Builders of Form or the Elohim (a Biblical words that many people think means "God," however it is a plural word). How do the Elohim create form, such as planet earth? They do so by using spiritual light that is stepped down in vibration, until it vibrates within the frequency spectrum of the material universe. In order to create the vast diversity seen in the material realm, several forms of spiritual light are combined. Once the light is in the right vibration, the Elohim together superimpose a mental image upon the light, and as the light coalesces around the image, a physical planet appears.

This is not an instantaneous process. The Biblical image of God creating the world in seven days is not meant to be understood literally as seven 24-hour periods. It is meant to represent seven cycles, each of which represents a particular form of spiritual light. There are seven Elohim who created the material planet, and they used seven different forms of spiritual light to do so. Each form of light is often referred to as a spiritual "ray," meaning there are seven rays that combined to create the physical universe.

This process is not as linear as the analytical mind would like to believe. It is not that first one ray was applied, then the second and so forth. The rays are not separate but are more like facets of a diamond, and the pure light of the Creator shines through them all at once. Only together do they form a complete picture, and only when they all work in oneness, will a form as complex as a planet or solar system be manifest. The following sections give a brief description of the seven rays.

First Ray

God Will and God Power. As the first step towards creating or co-creating, there has to be a will to project power out from oneself. For example, the Creator of the world of form is a self-contained and self-sufficient Being. The Creator was content to be what is was but still had the will to become *more* by creating a world of form and sending self-aware extensions of itself into it, so they could grow in awareness. As a spiritual person, it is easy to seek personal peace and create an environment in which one is comfortable. However, if one is not doing something to raise up all life, one will not grow beyond a certain point.

Many people have perverted God Power and are more than willing to project power in order to control others. Many spiritual people are beyond this, but it is easy to go into the opposite extreme and not be willing to project any power but think it is enough to be gentle and kind towards anyone. It should be noted that Jesus actively challenged the scribes and Pharisees in order to help awaken the people. Many spiritual people can get stuck on the beginning stages of the path because they are not willing to take the initiation of how to express God Power in a balanced manner. The masters who work on the First Ray are more than willing to help people learn this lesson and thus step on to the higher stages of the spiritual path. Until a student has passed the initiations of the First Ray, he or she cannot move on to the other rays, as one will not be given further initiations until one has proven that one can express power without misusing it.

Second Ray

God Wisdom. When one has summoned the will to co-create, the next step is to apply wisdom so that power can be expressed in a balanced manner that raises the All. The perversion of power is that it is expressed to raise the separate self in comparison to others, thus seeking to hold others back in order to raise oneself.

It takes wisdom to see through the illusions of the dualistic mind and instead tune in to the One Mind – often called the Christ mind – in order to know what will raise all and thus have maximum impact on one's own growth. The masters on the Second Ray will help anyone find this wisdom by going within instead of looking for outer knowledge in books or scriptures. An outer teaching can easily become a distraction and be seen as an end in itself. Ideally, the outer teaching only stimulates the intuitive faculties so that the student can use the "Key of Knowledge" to establish an inner connection to his or her higher self and thus to the masters of wisdom.

Third Ray

God Love. Many spiritual people think they are truly loving, but define it as always being soft-spoken and kind, never challenging other people. This is simply one dualistic polarity, and the opposite is possessive love that seeks to control other people. Divine Love is non-dualistic, meaning it has no conditions. One does not have to live up to any conditions in order to receive it.

One simply has to accept Divine Love or reject it, but when one is caught in the dualistic mind, one cannot accept unconditional love. One wants to define conditions for its expression instead of unconditionally accepting what is given freely.

The masters on the Third Ray seek to help people rise above conditional love – and both possessive love and the soft-spoken love are conditional – in order to become open doors for Divine Love to flow through their beings. This requires one to learn that when the population of an entire planet is trapped in duality, it is not truly loving to leave them alone or not to challenge their illusions. It was precisely by challenging people's illusions that Jesus demonstrated one aspect of Divine Love, namely that it will challenge any condition that keeps people from receiving itself.

Fourth Ray

God Purity and Discipline. The first three rays form a three-fold flame of Power, Wisdom and Love that corresponds to the Christian Trinity of Father, Son and Holy Spirit. This trinity is not complete in itself but needs to be balanced by the fourth element of purity, which corresponds to the Mother or Ma-ter element. The purity and discipline of the Fourth Ray are actually a special kind of wisdom, often called the Divine Sophia. It helps students understand how the material universe works and helps them build the discipline that prevents them from being tempted into expressing their co-creative powers for raising the separate self.

It is important to understand how free will works. A self-aware being has complete free will, meaning it can do or co-create anything it wants. However, it cannot avoid experiencing its own creation. This happens in the form of material circumstances, including physical diseases, and in the form of the co-creator living inside its own consciousness (experiencing the world through the filter or mental box it has created). Whereas a being has complete free will, any expression of will creates consequences that the being will experience in time and space—and this can indeed limit one's options. It takes wisdom and discipline to express one's co-creative abilities in such a way that one does not limit one's future choices. It is not an angry God that takes away your freedom, but the consequences of your own past choices. Without wisdom and discipline, one can easily create so many limitations that it takes lifetimes to uncreate them. The masters on the Fourth Ray are always willing to help students avoid this cycle of karma and rebirth.

Fifth Ray

God Truth and Healing. A person needs to reach a certain level of consciousness before he or she can recognize the existence and validity of a spiritual path that leads beyond the "normal" state of human consciousness. Even when a student finds the path, the student's motivation for wanting to follow the path is dependent upon the student's level of consciousness. Many people begin the spiritual path for the purpose of attaining something that will enhance their own lives. All people start the path for the purpose of gaining something for the separate self. This often springs from a desire to have certain powers, a desire to have extraordinary knowledge and wisdom or a desire to be more loving. While such desires are not wrong, they can be unbalanced and can thus take a student into various blind alleys that actually slow down the growth towards a non-dualistic state of consciousness. As a student begins to pass the initiations of the Fourth Ray, it also begins to gain a higher vision of life and its purpose. It learns to see the underlying reality that every aspect of life on earth has been distorted by the dualistic illusions. This at first gives rise to the recognition that all limiting circumstances – including physical and mental diseases and imbalances – are due to an unbalanced expression of one's co-creative abilities, which has given rise to a fragmented self. The true goal for the spiritual path is not to gain power, wisdom or love for that separate self but to transcend the separate self – which must be fragmented by nature – and attain a sense of self that is whole and self-sufficient. The true goal of the path is not power, wisdom or glory but wholeness. The student can then begin to work with the masters of the Fifth Ray in order to attain this personal wholeness.

As a degree of wholeness is attained, the student begins to glimpse another underlying reality, namely that all life is one, that reality is indivisible. The student broadens its sense of self to include all life, and this naturally gives rise to a desire to raise the All as the ultimate way to raise oneself.

Sixth Ray

God Service and Peace. When a student begins to see the underlying oneness of all life, it can move on to the Sixth Ray of service, of seeking to raise the All. The realization that all life is one also makes it clear that there can be no real conflicts between different expressions of the One Life. All conflict springs from the illusions of duality and separation, and the only way to bring true peace is to help people see through and rise above the entire dualistic mind and its veil of illusions. At this point, the student transcends all focus on itself as a separate being and focuses all of its attention on raising the All by exposing the dualistic illusions. This is what Jesus did, and that is why he is called the "Prince of Peace." Only those who truly see beyond duality can bring peace to this planet, which at this point is the most needed form of spiritual service. The masters of the Sixth Ray are here to help all people rise above the dualistic illusions and become emissaries of true, non-dualistic peace.

Seventh Ray

God Freedom. When one passes the initiations of the Sixth Ray, one attains true non-violence or non-aggression. Only the separate self can feel threatened by anything in the material universe—the reason being that it identifies itself as a material being. When a student rises to the initiations of the Seventh Ray, it begins to transcend all identification with the physical body or anything else in the material universe. It begins to reclaim its true identity as a spiritual being who is beyond the vibrations of the material realm and cannot be threatened or even affected (except through its own free-will choices) by any conditions in the material world. This is true spiritual freedom.

The fact that one becomes non-violent does not mean that one becomes passive. On the contrary, one becomes very active in seeking to set others free from duality. This is not done from the sense of a separate self that is subject to material conditions. It is done from a sense of a spiritual self that is free to flow with the directions from the spiritual realm. In any situation it can be the open door for setting others free.

Instead of being forced by the conditions of the separate self and the mass consciousness, one is now free to express one's Divine individuality and flow with the force that seeks to set all life free. This force is sometimes called the Holy Spirit and sometimes the River of Life. The masters on the Seventh Ray are ready to help students immerse themselves in this River of Life and eventually become one with it, thus attaining true freedom from all material conditions even while one is still in embodiment.

Chohans, Elohim and Archangels

Each ray has an ascended master who is the leader of the beings serving on that ray. This spiritual office is called a chohan. Each ray also has an Elohim and an archangel, both of which usually have divine consorts so they form a masculine-feminine polarity. There are, of course, many ascended masters serving on each ray. The following list shows the names of the Elohim, the Archangel and the chohan for the first seven rays.

- **First** Ray: Elohim Hercules and Amazonia. Archangel Michael and Faith. Master MORE.

- **Second** Ray: Elohim Apollo and Lumina. Archangel Jophiel and Christine. Lord Lanto.

- **Third** Ray: Elohim Heros and Amora. Archangel Chamuel and Charity. Paul the Venetian.

- **Fourth** Ray: Elohim Purity and Astrea. Archangel Gabriel and Hope. Serapis Bey.

- **Fifth** Ray: Elohim Cyclopea and Virginia. Archangel Raphael and Mother Mary. Hilarion.

- **Sixth** Ray: Elohim Peace and Aloha. Archangel Uriel and Aurora. Nada.

- **Seventh** Ray: Elohim Arcturus and Victoria. Archangel Zadkiel and Amethyst. Saint Germain and Kuan Yin.

The four levels of the material realm

In order to develop a higher approach to communication – and understand how the ascended masters give their teachings – it is necessary to take another look at the fact that everything is energy and that energy is a form of vibration. It is common knowledge that the human eye can detect only light that vibrates within a certain spectrum of frequencies, normally called visible light. It is also common knowledge that there are forms of light that vibrate at both lower and higher frequencies than visible light. For example, ultraviolet light has a higher frequency than visible violet light.

Light of different frequencies can interact and form an interference pattern, and the seven spiritual rays have combined, forming an interference pattern that makes up the material universe. As mentioned, spiritual light is gradually lowered in vibration until it vibrates in the spectrum of frequencies making up physical matter. Because physical matter is currently rather dense, there is a large gap in frequency between the matter realm and the lowest level of the spiritual realm. In this gap are three other realms, or frequency spectra, that represent successively lower vibrations, spanning the range from the spiritual to the physical realm. The energy waves of these three realms combine to make up physical matter. The three higher levels of the material realm also correspond to three levels of the human mind:

- **The etheric or identity realm.** This is the highest frequency spectrum in the material world, and it is the first realm that spiritual light "enters" as it is lowered in vibration. This is where the light begins to take on the forms that will eventually manifest as anything from galaxies to your physical body. At this level is stored the blueprint for all matter phenomena. For example,

the original and pure blueprint for planet earth is still
stored unchanged at this level. The pure blueprint for
your physical body is stored in your personal identity
body. The etheric level corresponds to the highest level
of the mind, the etheric or identity mind. As the name
implies, this is where your sense of identity is anchored.
As it is the highest level of the mind, it naturally affects
everything that comes after it. If you identify yourself
as a sinner, this sense of identity will inevitably affect
your thoughts and feelings about yourself and thus also
impact your actions.

• **The mental realm.** This is the level of thought
where the etheric blueprint takes on a more concrete
form. This level is denser than the identity level, meaning that the forms that exist here are less fluid and harder
to change than what is found above. For example, your
thoughts about yourself are more difficult to change than
your sense of identity. The mental level is more dense,
so thoughts are more solidified and harder to change at
that level. It is more efficient to go to the identity level
and change your sense of identity, which will automatically affect the thoughts that follow from it. The catch
is that unless you know about the levels of the mind, it
is difficult to attune your conscious mind to the higher
vibrations of the identity mind. The teachings and tools
in this book will help you do this.

• **The emotional realm.** This is obviously the level
of feelings, but emotions can also be seen as energy in
motion. This is the level right above the physical so this
is where the concrete thoughts in the mental realm are
imbued with the energy that is superimposed upon the

Ma-ter light and causes it to coalesce as a physical form. Although the emotions might seem fluid and volatile, it is actually quite difficult to change your emotions from the level of the emotional mind. Emotions are followers of thoughts so only by changing the thoughts can you truly overcome certain emotions. Only by changing your sense of identity can you take command over your thoughts.

The flow of energy in your mind

The lowest level of the mind is that of the conscious mind, and this is where you make conscious decisions about how to take physical action. In many cases your actions are not really the result of free conscious choices, as your decisions are based on what is presented to the conscious mind from the three higher levels of the mind. In order to illustrate this, compare it to a movie projector.

What drives your mental activity is a stream of energy that flows from your spiritual self or I AM Presence. This energy is like the white light produced by the light bulb in the movie projector. As the light enters your mind, it first passes through your identity mind, which can be compared to a film strip in the projector. Obviously, the light takes on the form of whatever images you have stored in your identity mind.

When the light has taken on the identity images, it now enters your mental body. It is as if you inserted a second film strip in the movie projector. The light will now take on a combination – an interference pattern – of the images in your identity and mental minds. You may have thoughts that reinforce your sense of identity or you may have thoughts that block your sense of identity. The combined pattern now enters your emotional body, which is like a third film strip. The emotional body serves as a storehouse for emotional energies. For example, many people have built a reservoir of the energies of anger and fear in their emotional bodies. As the light passes through these accumulations, it creates a new interference pattern that then enters the conscious mind.

By that time, the light has taken on the images and feelings stored in the higher levels of the mind, and it may appear to the conscious mind as an impulse that is so powerful that people immediately put it into actions or words. They either do not think there is any need to override it, or they do not feel they have the power to override it with their conscious minds. The result is that we often do or say things that we later regret.

What blocks communication from the heart

A lot of the communication between people is determined by the contents of peoples' outer minds, also called the four lower bodies. The outer mind is a very complex structure and it may contain many distorted beliefs and images. As one example, some people have subconscious beliefs that make them think they are constantly under threat. Anything you say to them will be seen as a threat, and their main concern is how to refute what you say or even stop you from saying anything. There is no way you can have a higher form of communication with such people. You might not feel you are communicating with a real person, as the conversation is at a surface level and never reaches the deeper level of the heart.

The ascended masters teach that many people are so identified with their outer minds that they actually think they *are* the mind or personality. In reality, we are spiritual beings who are only using the outer mind as a vehicle for expressing ourselves in the material world. You may be familiar with the concept that our spirits use the physical body as a vehicle for acting on earth.

The ascended masters teach that even the outer mind is a vehicle and that we are more than the mind.

To help us overcome identification with the outer mind, the ascended masters have given us the concept that the core of our identity is a self that has no identification with anything in the material world. The masters have called it the formless self or the Conscious You, but in the world's mystical traditions it has been called by other names, such as naked awareness, the pure self or the non-dual self.

The masters teach that the Conscious You has the ability to identify itself as anything it chooses. The Conscious You takes embodiment in the material world in order to accomplish two things, namely to help co-create this world and to experience this world. The Conscious You experiences this world through the outer self, the four lower bodies, and it also expresses its creative powers through this structure. Yet the Conscious You does not *become* the outer self.

The ascended masters teach that most people on earth are in a state of mind in which the Conscious You has forgotten its spiritual origin and nature. Instead, it has come to identify itself *with* or *as* the four lower bodies. The Conscious You can at any time start the process of awakening from the identification with the four lower bodies, and this is indeed the central aspect of the spiritual path or the path of self-mastery.

The path to higher communication

The ascended masters teach that many people are completely focused at the level of the physical body. The reason is that the Conscious You of such a person has come to identify itself with and as the physical body and the person's outer situation. Other people are focused on the emotional body and live their lives primarily through their emotions. Still other people are focused at the mental level and live their lives as intellectuals who are focused on knowledge and ideas.

Many spiritually interested people are focused at the identity level. We are beginning to realize that we are more than our physical bodies, our emotions and our thoughts. Our challenge is that we often still have beliefs in our four lower bodies that cause us to go into certain patterns of actions or communication. This is why we so often find it difficult to "walk our talk," meaning that we cannot live up to the spiritual ideals we know are real. The way to overcome this stage is to become aware that you are a formless being, call it the Conscious You or something else, and that you can separate yourself from any of the patterns in your four lower bodies. Separating yourself from all of these patterns is the key to reaching the highest goal of the spiritual path.

Obviously, the patterns in the four levels of the mind also affect our ability to communicate from the heart. If you feel threatened, it is not the pure being, that you truly are, who feels threatened. When the Conscious You is aware that it is a formless spiritual being, it cannot feel threatened by anything in the material universe because it knows that nothing in this world can affect it. The Conscious You is beyond the vibrations of the material world. If the Conscious You is identified with a pattern in, for example, the emotional body, then it will perceive a given situation through that pattern. You will be unable to respond to the situation as a spiritual being, but you respond as a limited being who feels threatened. If the other person does the same, you now have a conflict that will seem to have no resolution. The two people simply cannot communicate beyond their outer personalities.

The key to better communication is that you start becoming aware that you are a formless spiritual being. As you begin to feel less threatened by anything other people do or say, you will be able to speak from the level of the heart. This is really the level of your higher or spiritual self, what the ascended masters call your I AM Presence. This self resides in the higher vibrations of the spiritual realm and it never feels threatened by anything in this world. Your I AM Presence only has one goal, namely to raise up all people.

When you speak from the level of your I AM Presence, your communication always seeks to raise up others. Some people will be able to sense this and they will respond in a way that suddenly resolves a situation that previously seemed to have no solution. Other people will not respond, but you can then avoid reacting negatively and this will often set you free from such people so you can move on with your life.

Communication and the seven rays

The connection between the seven spiritual rays and communication is that all of the patterns in your four lower bodies are created by taking the qualities of the rays and giving them a lower vibration and focus. Each of the patterns that block communication from your spiritual self is created by taking some quality of a spiritual ray and perverting it by focusing it on the perception and the needs of the separate self.

As a specific example, the First Ray of power can be perverted so that people feel they always have to be right. Such people go into a conversation with the underlying fear that they could be proven wrong. They evaluate everything said by others based on the fear of being proven wrong, meaning that they often do not hear what other people are actually saying. Instead, they are so focused on refuting anything that seems like a threat that they cannot connect to other people at a deeper level. They cannot have a genuine conversation with others because it all happens at a superficial level. There are numerous patterns that block genuine communication, but they are all created by per-verting one of the seven spiritual rays. The key to spiritualizing your communication skills is to gradually become aware of the patterns in your four lower bodies.

It is the Conscious You that has this ability. The Conscious You can step outside your four lower bodies and become aware that you have a pattern that causes you to always respond in a certain way. The Conscious You can come to see this response as limiting and it can then come to the realization: "But I am not this pattern; I am more than the pattern." Through this process the Conscious You – *you* – come to stop identifying itself with the pattern and instead begins to shift its identity towards the I AM Presence. This process is the key to spiritual growth. "I am not this pattern down here, I am the spiritual being up there."

The following chapters and their corresponding exercises are designed to help you speed up the process whereby you become aware of how the perversions of the seven rays limit your communication. By studying the discourses and giving the invocations, you will accomplish two things:

• You will gradually transform the energy misqualified through a certain belief. This energy is accumulated in your four lower bodies and it pulls the Conscious You into identifying itself with the outer personality.

• You will become more conscious of the pattern and thus start the process that leads to the Conscious You finally seeing the pattern from the outside and thus experiencing that it is more than the pattern.

The ascended masters have themselves gone through the process of overcoming identification with their own outer minds. They are very skilled at helping us do the same. Allow the masters to take you through the gradual process of refining your communication skills by learning to make the highest possible use of the seven spiritual rays.

2 | TAKING RESPONSIBILITY
FOR YOUR MIND

*A dictation by Master MORE, representing the First Ray
of God's will and power.*

I greet you in the flame of MORE that I AM. But why
am I one with that flame, my beloved? Because I made
a choice to be one with that flame, I made a choice to
acknowledge who I AM. You, then, are also making
choices, for life is a series of choices.

There are those on earth who deny that they have free
will. But it is not the Spirit who denies this, for it can
only be the ego that denies it. The ego does not want the
Conscious You – the Spirit – to make choices. It wants
to maintain control, and thus it will not allow the conscious self to make the choice to acknowledge that it has
choices. The ego will not allow the self to acknowledge,
for example, that it has the choice to go beyond the limitations of the body, or even the identification with the body
in which so many people are trapped—believing they are
nothing more than matter.

This is the difference between those who are still
asleep and those who are beginning to awaken. How

do you awaken? You awaken by recognizing that you have a choice—instead of falling into the pattern that you hear so many people express: "I had no choice," or "I had no *other* choice" than doing what I did.

There is always a choice

When you hear a person make this statement, you know that this person has not been willing to take responsibility for his or her life, for his or her situation. For when you do take that responsibility, you recognize the very fact that no matter what the outer circumstances might be, you always have a choice to adjust your state of mind and choose a different reaction to those circumstances than what might be the standard reaction among 99 percent of the people living on this planet—and what might indeed be the standard reaction that has been programmed into your mind since childhood.

There are those, my beloved, who have perverted the teachings of Christ to the point where they do not recognize that the essence of Jesus' teachings was that you have choices. Did Christ not say: "Resist not evil. Turn the other cheek."

Well, is it not so that most people on this planet have been programmed to resist evil and to give back in kind—to respond in kind? Do you not see that the essence of the teachings of Christ is that you have the potential, the ability, to choose to turn the other cheek—even when someone strikes you on one cheek?

Communicating from the heart

This relates very much to the topic of this book. Why am I opening this book? Because I am the chohan of the First Ray of the Will of God. How do you begin to communicate from the heart? Well, you must decide that you are willing to communicate from the heart. You must choose, you must make a decision, that you are willing to communicate from the heart.

Many of you will instantly say that you are willing to communicate from the heart. But you do not always realize how you have been programmed throughout your lives to not communicate from the heart. You do not always realize how difficult it may be to step back from this programming and indeed communicate at a deeper level.

This is the reality we all face when we are in physical embodiment. What is the level at which we choose to communicate? Is it the pre-programmed response where we respond to a certain situation by giving back in kind or by reinforcing choices that were made earlier—perhaps in childhood, perhaps in past lifetimes? In that case, we are not actually making a conscious choice. We are allowing our past choices to repeat themselves without truly taking a stand for who we are.

The choice you face is whether to communicate from the outer personality or whether to communicate from the inner personality. You can only communicate from the inner personality through the heart. You cannot communicate from the inner personality through the mind alone. You can let the mind be an expression of the heart but you cannot – with the mind itself – communicate from the inner personality.

The reality of oneness

You cannot analyze communication from the heart, break it down into components and attempt to imitate them with the outer, linear, analytical mind. My beloved, it cannot be done because of one very simple fact: Communication from the heart is based on the reality of oneness. There is no other way to communicate from the heart than by being in oneness, by surrendering to oneness, by working for the oneness of All—whereby you seek to raise up the All. You cannot communicate from the heart unless you have made the decision that oneness is more important than separation.

When you look at the world – when you look at how people communicate – you see that so much of the communication that goes on is not based on the reality – the recognition – of oneness. It is based on one person seeking to raise him- or herself up compared to others, seeking to control others, seeking to avoid being hurt by others, seeking to tear others down by criticizing, by judging, by imposing a standard based on the false belief that if you live up to an outer standard on earth, you are guaranteed entry into the kingdom of God that is beyond earth—which, of course, cannot happen. How can you use that which has separated you from the kingdom of God to enter the kingdom of God? It is – naturally – not possible, my beloved.

The very foundation for communicating from the heart is to realize that it must be based on a recognition of the oneness of all life. Which means that when you communicate with another person, your intent, your goal, your desire is to raise up that person.

Self-awareness

How do you avoid judging, how do you avoid criticizing, how do you avoid blaming, how do you avoid comparing that person to some standard that you have in your mind of what you think is best for that person? Consider that the First Ray is the ray of the Will of God and the Power of God. When you come to contemplate the will of God, you recognize that the ultimate will of God is to create self-aware extensions of itself. But what is self-awareness? Well, you cannot have self-awareness without having free will.

If the self does not have the ability to choose, it is not a self—it has no identity, it cannot choose what it will be. You will notice that when Moses on the mountain asked God to give him a name, God said: "Yod He Wav He—I will Be who I will Be." Not the "I AM that I AM," as is so often translated. The reality is that God did not give Moses a name because God is the ever self-transcending Being. God said: "I reserve the right to be who I will be at any moment."

This is the essence of free will—that you choose who you will be at any moment. This is where you must begin to communicate from the heart—by choosing who you will be in relation to the person or persons with whom you are communicating. Will you choose to be trapped in the illusion of the separate self—that you are separate from them, that you might be in opposition to them, that they might hurt you, that they might threaten you? Or that you need to control them for their own good—for you know best?

You see, when you choose to be the separate self, you cannot respect the free will of other people. If you do not respect free will – and when I say "respect" I mean complete, unconditional acceptance – then you cannot actually experience oneness with others.

Oneness cannot be forced. Oneness cannot come about as the result of force or control. Oneness must be based on a complete, unconditional acceptance of the Creator's decision to create extensions of itself, give them individuality and give them free will. Thereby, they have the potential to choose—to be more, to be less, to be this, to be that.

Your highest potential

This is the sublime – the supreme – decision of your Creator. When you understand and accept this fully and totally, then you can be in oneness with the Creator—the Creator's intent, the Creator's purpose of not forcing or programming people to be raised up to a certain standard. Instead allowing beings the free will and the space to choose to Be *more*, to choose to come into oneness with each other, to choose to come into oneness with their source.

This is the plan of salvation of your Living God, your living Creator. What has happened is, of course, that certain beings in an unascended sphere that has since ascended chose to rebel against that plan and that decision. They chose to use their free will to rebel against it. They entered into the consciousness of separation that is a potential when you have free will. They have since taken over the collective mind of the beings who embody on this planet and certain other planets throughout the galaxies (but your concern should be primarily this one, as you are stuck here until you learn the lessons and decide to take back your free will).

In order to take back your own free will and truly make free choices, you must come to respect the Creator's decision, the Creator's choice, to give you and all other self-aware beings free will. Only when you respect the free will of others, can you truly accept your own free will and your own right to choose to Be *more*, even though yesterday you might have chosen to be *less*.

The ultimate lie of the false teachers is that once you have chosen a lesser identity, you cannot simply let go of it, you cannot abandon it, you cannot rise above it. When you understand free will, you understand – you accept, you experience – that you have the right to say with your God: "I will Be who I will Be." Therefore, you can choose to let go of that old identity, to let it die, to let it vanish, to let it go into the flame that you are.

This is your highest potential, my beloved—to choose to be *more* than you were a second ago. This is the only way to overcome the blocks to communication, the way that is based on oneness and seeks to raise all life instead of seeking to tear down.

Respecting the free will of others and your freedom

When you truly accept free will and the wisdom of the Creator's choice, you recognize that God gave each individual being the right to choose what they will be. When you meet another with whom you might have had conflicts in the past, when you accept free will, you accept that the person has an absolute God-given right to be in the state of consciousness in which that person in currently abiding. This is their right, my beloved. God has given them that right.

Unless you have fallen prey to the illusion of the fallen beings – that you know better than God – you should accept that God has given them that right. You accept that whatever state of consciousness they are in, they are exercising their God-given right of free will, which gives them the right to choose to be anything they want to be. Yet God has also set up a material universe that will, so to speak, make sure that they actually experience the state of consciousness in which they are choosing to be, even the physical manifestations of that state of consciousness, as everything is the manifestation of consciousness.

When you understand and accept this, you do not need to judge them. You do not need to have a standard in your head for how you think they should be. You can set them free to be who they will be at that moment.

How can you set them free? Well, by giving equal acceptance to your own free will that you give to theirs. When you accept that they have a right to be in that particular state of consciousness, you also accept that you have a right to be in any state of consciousness that you choose. You have complete freedom to choose your state of consciousness independently of the choices made by any other human being, even independently of the collective choice made by every human being on earth.

This is what Jesus demonstrated. Despite the fact that all of the people he met during that embodiment had chosen not to be in the Christ consciousness, he still had the right to choose to be in the Christ consciousness, to be the Christ and to demonstrate it.

When you understand that you do not need to let other people's choices influence *your* choices, then you will have the blending of the Alpha and Omega where you can set others free and set yourself free at the same time. This means that when you interact with another, then you know that regardless of their state of consciousness, you can choose your own state of consciousness. You can communicate with that person based on your free-will choice of a certain state of consciousness—without feeling that their state of consciousness, their words, are forcing you to respond in a certain way.

A common cause of conflict

Much of the conflict between human beings is precisely due to the fact that so many people believe that when they encounter another person – who does not behave or speak to them the way they think they should be spoken to – then their only option is to go into a negative frame of mind—be it fear, be it anger or any other negative emotion. The Spirit immediately feels trapped by having to go into that negative reaction. But if it does not fully accept free will or take responsibility for itself, then it will blame the other person for forcing it to go into a negative state of mind—instead of acknowledging the reality that it is making the choice to enter that negative frame of mind. You need to acknowledge that you could just as easily choose a different reaction, a higher reaction, a reaction based on love rather than fear and one of the many shades of fear. Truly, all negative reactions and emotions spring from the fear that comes from separation.

The key to overcoming all of these negative emotions – the key to avoiding the trap of going into these emotions – is indeed to step back and say to yourself: "I can choose oneness even if that person has chosen separation! The fact that another person has chosen to see him- or herself separated from me – to see me as an enemy, as an opponent, as a threat – does not mean that I have to make the same choice. I can choose oneness! I can first of all choose oneness with my own inner being whereby I go within, in my inner sanctuary."

Your inner sanctuary

This inner sanctuary, my beloved, you should all be aware of. For the pearl of great price can be seen as the secret chamber of your heart, which is the very core of your heart. Certainly, when we say "heart," you realize we are not speaking about the physical organ that pumps blood, but about the heart chakra and the very core behind it—that point that is so infinitely small that it could never be found by any amount of material digging and even the best microscopes constructed by science.

You need to realize that there is that point within you, that point that is the meeting ground between the material and the spiritual realm. That is the core of your being where you can always retreat and re-establish your oneness with your own higher being. You should not only see it as a point, but work on making it a sphere that you expand and expand and expand— until it extends way beyond your physical body and your energy field so that you are always enveloped in that sphere and nothing can actually come in and touch your outer mind, even the analytical mind.

Once you retreat into that inner sanctum, connect to the oneness with your own higher being and realize who you are, then you can choose a different reaction than a standard, programmed response that you have grown up, perhaps over many lifetimes, to give in certain situations.

You are not a robot

My beloved, think back to what I said in the beginning about the people who deny that they have free will. What is the implication of this? If you do not have free will, you are an automaton, you are a robot, you are a machine. What is the essence of a machine? If you push a certain button, you are guaranteed to get a certain reaction from the machine. If you do not get that reaction, the machine is not working correctly—there is something wrong, something that needs to be fixed.

You are a creative being. The fact that someone pushes your buttons does not mean that you have to respond in a negative way—for you can choose not to be a computer. You can choose to be a co-creator, and you can co-create a better response by reconnecting to your own higher being and realizing that – certainly – your I AM Presence – who is beyond anything in the material world – cannot be affected by somebody else being in a bad mood. It would never respond in a negative way to other people—no matter what they do to you.

When you establish that oneness, then you have a foundation for co-creating with your higher self a positive response, an uplifting response, a response that seeks to uplift the other person rather than defend yourself or attack back and seek to tear the other person down, silence them or whatever responses you see repeated over and over and over again.

To be more, or not to be more

The question really is – in any situation you encounter, no matter what other people do or say – the question is: Do you want to be *more* in that situation? Or do you want to be less—meaning that you allow the other person or your own ego or the mass consciousness to control you and force you to be less than you truly are, as the infinitely creative co-creator that you are created to be. This is the choice—choose ye this day whom you will serve. Will you serve the lesser? Will you serve the *more?*

If you serve the *more*, then respect that God has given you that free will to choose to be *more* in any situation. When most people choose to be less, they do indeed form that self-reinforcing downward spiral that can cause humankind to go into the great depression, as it was called in the 1930s.

Consider that psychologically – emotionally, spiritually – humankind has been engaged in something we might call the great depression from a spiritual level. People have been engaged in it for a very long time—thinking that they are powerless, that there are certain limitations they cannot go beyond. They do not recognize the very reality that all is an expression of consciousness and that all elements of consciousness are the result of choices that you make. The choice is whether to accept this or that as part of your consciousness, as part of your identity, whether to accept that this is who I will be today, thereby implying that you are not being more than the identity that feels trapped in the material universe.

The high and the low potential

Where am I going with all this rambling? I am seeking to get you to the point where you realize that this book, and the process of using it, has a high and a low potential. It can be just another spiritual book where you feel good and you end up feeling lighter and you say: "Oh, that was great" and then you go right back to your old momentums and your old habit patterns. Or you can choose to make it an absolutely life-changing experience whereby you come up to a higher level, from which there is no way back. You have so firmly planted your feet on the rock of Christ within you that you know you cannot – you will not – go back to these old patterns and momentums. This is the choice you have every time you read a spiritual book. But I tell you that at this particular time it is more important than at any time in the past to consider that choice, to consider that potential.

Now I, of course, am an ascended being. I am in no way, shape or form threatened by the choices you make—nor do I have any desire whatsoever to control you. We of the ascended masters – as opposed to many of the beings who channel through various channelers – need nothing from you. We don't need your money, we don't need your attention, we don't need your energy, we don't need your obedience, we don't need you to worship us.

I am a God-free Being, my beloved, and in so being, I can set you free to be whatever you choose to be. I have no desire to influence your choice, but I do indeed have a right – a God-given right – to make you more aware that you have the potential to make a different choice. This is also what you have a right to do to anyone you encounter.

Break the old patterns

Certainly, I am not here talking about being tolerant or accepting of people being in a lesser state of mind. When you realize that you do not have to go down into their state of mind, you are automatically – so to speak – confronting them with the fact that there is a higher choice. They expect you to go into a negative reaction, which then reinforces whatever belief they have, whether they believe that you can be controlled through fear, or whether they believe that you can be controlled into going into anger by being provoked.

Whatever it may be, when you make the choice you have always made and go into the old patterns, you are reinforcing their image of you and your image of yourself as being lesser. But when you do choose a different reaction – a higher reaction – you are shocking the other person into realizing that something happened that has never happened before, something is new, something is different.

This is our primary purpose for speaking through messengers. It is to simply make people aware that there is a higher state of consciousness, that it is possible to ascend beyond the duality consciousness, the human ego, and all of the many patterns that it repeats over and over and over again.

There is a different choice to make. You can choose to be more than a human being, to be more than a pre-programmed biological robot—a biological computer that can only respond in certain ways when certain buttons are pushed. You can indeed choose to systematically resolve those buttons – those hang-ups, those wounds, those attachments – to the point where you have no buttons that the prince of this world can push. He has nothing in you whereby he can control you.

This is freedom, my beloved—the only way to be free on planet earth. It is the only way to be free *of* planet earth and ascend to a higher realm.

False students

There are indeed those – even those who call themselves ascended master students, having followed this or that dispensation – who have studied the teachings we gave—the teachings about *more*, the teachings about making better choices. They have turned them into a very subtle belief and belief system that if only you fulfill these outer requirements – by giving decrees, or going to services, or going to conferences, or studying books, or talking a certain way, or dressing a certain way, and not driving a red car, and all of this outer stuff – then you will be guaranteed to one day ascend. They think that one day, somehow, magically – "poof" – they will have ascended, without them having to face their egos and to choose to be *more* by choosing to look at the illusions of the ego and undoing them by choosing the reality of Christ rather than the dualistic illusion.

There is no automatic way to ascend, for the ascension is a choice! There is an ultimate choice, but before you rise to the level where you can make that choice to ascend, you must make many, many choices. Did not my beloved brother, Saint Germain, say that his ascension was the result of more than a million right choices where he chose to be *more* rather than to be less? This does not mean that Saint Germain took some kind of quiz, some kind of test, on earth. There is no multiple-choice test that can secure your ascension. It is creative choices we are talking about, and what is creativity? It is that which is *more*. This is the simplest definition of creativity you will ever find. That which is *more—that* is creativity.

True creativity

A creative choice is when you choose to be *more*—and when you choose to be more than that other person who wants you to fall back into the old patterns of less. You choose not to accept that and to, instead, be *more* and to express it, whereby you indeed rise above it and demonstrate that there is more to life than repeating these same old patterns of gossip, or quarreling or arguing. One must wonder how people can find any form of fulfillment or satisfaction in living a life where they mindlessly repeat these old patterns as a broken record.

Think about it, my beloved! Think about a broken record that many of you might have heard as children—even though some of you have grown up at a time when records have long been put on a shelf to collect dust. Think about how you know that a song is meant to progress, and when it repeats, how long does it take for your mind to realize that this is not right? How long does it take for your mind to feel a certain stress of wanting things to move on?

Well, do you not see that your mind is designed to be creative, and thus there is an aspect of your mind that cannot be satisfied by this life that has become a broken record—except for those who have been caught in the many versions of the catch-22 designed by the false teachers. These are people who cannot tune in to this desire to move on and therefore cannot free themselves from these endless patterns of repetition. But you *can*, or you would not be here—or you would not even be able to hear this message, my beloved. And you know it.

The turning point and your choice to be

That is why I say, again: You have come to a point where you have the potential to truly rise to an entirely different level and to make the reading of this book the absolute turning point in your personal life. Everything is in place. It is all there. It is all there. All that is needed is you making that choice and reinforcing the choice in the times to come so that whatever happens you will not go down even if the rest of humankind goes down into a spiral of fear, be it over the economy or war or whatever else might come. You have brought yourself to the point where you have the potential to permanently put yourself beyond the downward pull of the collective consciousness. No matter what happens in the outer, you will not even be tempted to go into a downward spiral, but you will continue to move upwards and upwards, always choosing to be *more*, no matter what the situation might be—be it in your personal lives or on a planetary scale.

This is where you are at. You are at the point that people were at when Jesus walked up to them and said: "Leave your nets and follow me, and I will make you fishers of men." You are ready to leave your nets, and we will make you fishers of men who can show people that there is indeed *more*.

Choose freely. Do not make a hasty choice with the outer mind. Use the process of reading this book to go within, to contact the inner core of your being. If you make a choice with the outer mind, you will have to battle the forces of this world who will oppose your choice.

Take the time. Take the time to go within until you reconnect to that moment where your very being chose to descend into this world to bring the light and the unconditional love of God. That is the choice—the spontaneous, completely unified, unconditional choice that nothing in this world can oppose. Only when you choose from *that* level of your being, will it be a sustainable choice, will it be a permanent choice. Only then will you *be*, will you have risen above the anti-Being.

When we of the ascended masters offer our sponsorship of a teaching or movement, it is not in an automatic way, as some of our previous students have believed, but in a creative way. We will not sponsor or reinforce the choices made with the outer mind. We will not reinforce your efforts to mechanically turn yourself into a person who seems to be spiritual by following outer rules. We will indeed reinforce your creative choices, the choices made from that point of oneness.

This is my vow, this is my offering to you on this day. I give you the complete freedom of my unconditional love to choose. Whatever you choose, you have my unconditional love. If that were not the case, then my love would not be unconditional, and then I would not be an ascended master. You become ascended by becoming free, and you set yourself free by setting all life free to choose, as is their God-given right.

My gratitude for your attention, my gratitude for your willingness to be the open doors for this release that has gone far into the mass consciousness of this planet. It has indeed sent shock waves into the denial of choice, the unwillingness to choose, the unwillingness to make a choice that is a real choice and not a preprogrammed response. This is the consciousness that I aim to break up. Again, my gratitude, and I seal you, my beloved, in the flame of God's Will—that is the will of the God within you, the God that you *are*.

3 | I INVOKE
UNCONDITIONAL WILL

In the name I AM THAT I AM, Jesus Christ, I call to my I AM Presence to flow through the I Will Be Presence that I AM and give this invocation with full power. I call to beloved Elohim Hercules and Amazonia, Archangel Michael and Faith, and Master MORE to help me overcome all blocks to my determination to communicate from the heart in all situations. Help me be free from all patterns or forces within or without that oppose my communication from the heart and my oneness with my I AM Presence, including ...

[Make personal calls]

1. I will communicate from the heart

1. I acknowledge who I AM. I am a self-aware being, a Conscious You, and I make the choice to acknowledge that I have choices.

> O Hercules Blue, you fill every space,
> with infinite Power and infinite Grace,
> you embody the key to creativity,
> the will to transcend into Infinity.

> **O Hercules Blue, in oneness with thee,**
> **I open my heart to your reality,**
> **in feeling your flame, so clearly I see,**
> **transcending my self is the true alchemy.**

2. I make the choice to go beyond the limitations of the body and the outer mind. I take full responsibility for my outer and inner situation.

> O Hercules Blue, I lovingly raise,
> my voice in giving God infinite praise,
> I'm grateful for playing my personal part,
> In God's infinitely intricate work of art.

> **O Hercules Blue, all life now you heal,**
> **enveloping all in your Blue-flame Seal,**
> **your electric-blue fire within us reveal,**
> **our innermost longing for all that is real.**

3. I recognize and accept that no matter what the outer circumstances might be, I always have a choice to adjust my state of mind and choose a different reaction to those circumstances.

O Hercules Blue, I pledge now my life,
in helping this planet transcend human strife,
duality's lies are pierced by your light,
restoring the fullness of my inner sight.

O Hercules Blue, I'm one with your will,
all space in my being with Blue Flame you fill,
your power allows me to forge on until,
I pierce every veil and climb every hill.

4. I am free from the collective programming to resist evil and to give back in kind. I take back my ability to turn the other cheek.

O Hercules Blue, your Temple of Light,
revealed to us all through our inner sight,
a beacon that radiates light to the earth,
bringing about our planet's rebirth.

O Hercules Blue, all life you defend,
giving us power to always transcend,
in you the expansion of self has no end,
as I in God's infinite spirals ascend.

5. I choose, I make the decision, that I am willing to communicate from the heart.

O Hercules Blue, you fill every space,
with infinite Power and infinite Grace,
you embody the key to creativity,
the will to transcend into Infinity.

O Hercules Blue, in oneness with thee,
I open my heart to your reality,
in feeling your flame, so clearly I see,
transcending my self is the true alchemy.

6. I will be conscious of the level at which I communicate. I will no longer communicate based on a pre-programmed response that reinforces past choices. I will make a conscious choice so that past choices do not repeat themselves.

O Hercules Blue, I lovingly raise,
my voice in giving God infinite praise,
I'm grateful for playing my personal part,
In God's infinitely intricate work of art.

O Hercules Blue, all life now you heal,
enveloping all in your Blue-flame Seal,
your electric-blue fire within us reveal,
our innermost longing for all that is real.

7. I am taking a stand for who I am. I will no longer communicate from the outer personality. I will communicate from the inner personality, from the heart.

> O Hercules Blue, I pledge now my life,
> in helping this planet transcend human strife,
> duality's lies are pierced by your light,
> restoring the fullness of my inner sight.

> **O Hercules Blue, I'm one with your will,**
> **all space in my being with Blue Flame you fill,**
> **your power allows me to forge on until,**
> **I pierce every veil and climb every hill.**

8. Communication from the heart is based on the reality of oneness. I communicate by being in oneness, by surrendering to oneness, by working for the oneness of All. I make the decision that oneness is more important than separation.

> O Hercules Blue, your Temple of Light,
> revealed to us all through our inner sight,
> a beacon that radiates light to the earth,
> bringing about our planet's rebirth.

> **O Hercules Blue, all life you defend,**
> **giving us power to always transcend,**
> **in you the expansion of self has no end,**
> **as I in God's infinite spirals ascend.**

9. Communicating from the heart is based on a recognition of the oneness of all life. When I communicate with another person, my intent, my goal, my desire is to raise up that person and all life.

> Accelerate into Creativity, I AM real,
> Accelerate into Creativity, all life heal,
> Accelerate into Creativity, I AM MORE,
> Accelerate into Creativity, all will soar.
>
> Accelerate into Creativity! (3X)
> Beloved Hercules and Amazonia.
> Accelerate into Creativity! (3X)
> Beloved Michael and Faith.
> Accelerate into Creativity! (3X)
> Beloved Master MORE.
> Accelerate into Creativity! (3X)
> Beloved I AM.

2. I accept free will

1. I acknowledge that I cannot have self-awareness without having free will. I accept that in every situation it is my responsibility to chose with God: "I will be who I will be."

> Michael Archangel, in your flame so blue,
> there is no more night, there is only you.
> In oneness with you, I am filled with your light,
> what glorious wonder, revealed to my sight.

> **Michael Archangel, your Faith is so strong,**
> **Michael Archangel, oh sweep me along.**
> **Michael Archangel, I'm singing your song,**
> **Michael Archangel, with you I belong.**

2. The essence of free will is that I choose who I will be at any moment. I communicate from the heart by choosing who I will be in relation to the people with whom I am communicating.

> Michael Archangel, protection you give,
> within your blue shield, I ever shall live.
> Sealed from all creatures, roaming the night,
> I remain in your sphere, of electric blue light.

> **Michael Archangel, your Faith is so strong,**
> **Michael Archangel, oh sweep me along.**
> **Michael Archangel, I'm singing your song,**
> **Michael Archangel, with you I belong.**

3. I will no longer be trapped in the illusion of the separate self that I am separate from other people or that I need to control them for their own good.

> Michael Archangel, what power you bring,
> as millions of angels, praises will sing.
> Consuming the demons, of doubt and of fear,
> I know that your Presence, will always be near.
>
> **Michael Archangel, your Faith is so strong,**
> **Michael Archangel, oh sweep me along.**
> **Michael Archangel, I'm singing your song,**
> **Michael Archangel, with you I belong.**

4. I choose to experience oneness with others by respecting their free will through complete, unconditional acceptance of the Creator's decision to create extensions of itself, give them individuality and give them free will.

> Michael Archangel, God's will is your love,
> you bring to us all, God's light from Above.
> God's will is to see, all life taking flight,
> transcendence of self, our most sacred right.
>
> **Michael Archangel, your Faith is so strong,**
> **Michael Archangel, oh sweep me along.**
> **Michael Archangel, I'm singing your song,**
> **Michael Archangel, with you I belong.**

5. I AM in oneness with my Creator, my Creator's intent, my Creator's purpose of not forcing or programming people to be raised up to a certain standard. I allow people the free will and the space to choose to Be *more*.

> Michael Archangel, in your flame so blue,
> there is no more night, there is only you.
> In oneness with you, I am filled with your light,
> what glorious wonder, revealed to my sight.

> **Michael Archangel, your Faith is so strong,**
> **Michael Archangel, oh sweep me along.**
> **Michael Archangel, I'm singing your song,**
> **Michael Archangel, with you I belong.**

6. I take back my own free will by respecting my Creator's decision to give all self-aware beings free will. I respect the free will of others, and I accept my own free will, my right to choose to Be *more*.

> Michael Archangel, protection you give,
> within your blue shield, I ever shall live.
> Sealed from all creatures, roaming the night,
> I remain in your sphere, of electric blue light.

> **Michael Archangel, your Faith is so strong,**
> **Michael Archangel, oh sweep me along.**
> **Michael Archangel, I'm singing your song,**
> **Michael Archangel, with you I belong.**

7. I accept, I experience, that I have the right to say with my God: "I will Be who I will Be." I choose to let go of the old identity, to let it die, to let it vanish, to let it go into the flame that I AM.

> Michael Archangel, what power you bring,
> as millions of angels, praises will sing.
> Consuming the demons, of doubt and of fear,
> I know that your Presence, will always be near.

> **Michael Archangel, your Faith is so strong,**
> **Michael Archangel, oh sweep me along.**
> **Michael Archangel, I'm singing your song,**
> **Michael Archangel, with you I belong.**

8. I truly accept free will and the wisdom of the Creator's choice. I accept that other people have an absolute God-given right to be in the state of consciousness they choose. I accept that God has given them that right.

> Michael Archangel, God's will is your love,
> you bring to us all, God's light from Above
> God's will is to see, all life taking flight,
> transcendence of self, our most sacred right.

> **Michael Archangel, your Faith is so strong,**
> **Michael Archangel, oh sweep me along.**
> **Michael Archangel, I'm singing your song,**
> **Michael Archangel, with you I belong.**

9. I accept that I do not need to judge other people. I set them free to be who they will be. I also give equal acceptance to my own free will. I accept that I have a right to be in any state of consciousness that I choose. I have freedom to choose my state of consciousness independently of the choices made by other people.

> With angels I soar,
> as I reach for MORE.
> The angels so real,
> their love all will heal.
> The angels bring peace,
> all conflicts will cease.
> With angels of light,
> we soar to new height.

> **The rustling sound of angel wings,**
> **what joy as even matter sings,**
> **what joy as every atom rings,**
> **in harmony with angel wings.**

3. I make higher choices

1. I accept that I have the right to make the choice made by Jesus. Even if all other people I meet have chosen not to be in the Christ consciousness, I still have the right to choose to be in the Christ consciousness, to *be* the Christ and to demonstrate it.

O Hercules Blue, you fill every space,
with infinite Power and infinite Grace,
you embody the key to creativity,
the will to transcend into Infinity.

O Hercules Blue, in oneness with thee,
I open my heart to your reality,
in feeling your flame, so clearly I see,
transcending my self is the true alchemy.

2. When I interact with other people, I know that regardless of their state of consciousness, I can choose my own state of consciousness. I can communicate with people based on my free-will choice without feeling forced to respond in a certain way.

O Hercules Blue, I lovingly raise,
my voice in giving God infinite praise,
I'm grateful for playing my personal part,
In God's infinitely intricate work of art.

O Hercules Blue, all life now you heal,
enveloping all in your Blue-flame Seal,
your electric-blue fire within us reveal,
our innermost longing for all that is real.

3. I know that when I encounter people who do not behave or speak as I expect, it is not my only option to go into a negative frame of mind. I will choose a different reaction, a higher reaction, a reaction based on love rather than the fear that comes from separation.

> O Hercules Blue, I pledge now my life,
> in helping this planet transcend human strife,
> duality's lies are pierced by your light,
> restoring the fullness of my inner sight.

> **O Hercules Blue, I'm one with your will,**
> **all space in my being with Blue Flame you fill,**
> **your power allows me to forge on until,**
> **I pierce every veil and climb every hill.**

4. In tense situations I will step back and say to myself: "I can choose oneness even if that person has chosen separation! The fact that another person has chosen to see himself or herself separated from me – to see me as an enemy, as an opponent, as a threat – does not mean that I have to make the same choice. I can choose oneness with my own inner being whereby I go within, in my inner sanctuary."

> O Hercules Blue, your Temple of Light,
> revealed to us all through our inner sight,
> a beacon that radiates light to the earth,
> bringing about our planet's rebirth.

> **O Hercules Blue, all life you defend,**
> **giving us power to always transcend,**
> **in you the expansion of self has no end,**
> **as I in God's infinite spirals ascend.**

5. I acknowledge the point within me that is the meeting ground between the material and the spiritual realm. I retreat into the core of my being to establish oneness with my I AM Presence. I am enveloped in the sphere of my Presence and nothing can touch my mind.

O Hercules Blue, you fill every space,
with infinite Power and infinite Grace,
you embody the key to creativity,
the will to transcend into Infinity.

O Hercules Blue, in oneness with thee,
I open my heart to your reality,
in feeling your flame, so clearly I see,
transcending my self is the true alchemy.

6. I retreat into my inner sanctum, connect to the oneness with my I AM Presence and accept who I AM. I choose a different reaction than the standard, programmed response that I have developed over many lifetimes.

O Hercules Blue, I lovingly raise,
my voice in giving God infinite praise,
I'm grateful for playing my personal part,
In God's infinitely intricate work of art.

O Hercules Blue, all life now you heal,
enveloping all in your Blue-flame Seal,
your electric-blue fire within us reveal,
our innermost longing for all that is real.

7. I am a creative being. I choose to be a co-creator. I co-create a better response by reconnecting to my I AM Presence who is beyond anything in the material world. I will not respond in a negative way to other people, no matter what they do to me.

O Hercules Blue, I pledge now my life,
in helping this planet transcend human strife,
duality's lies are pierced by your light,
restoring the fullness of my inner sight.

**O Hercules Blue, I'm one with your will,
all space in my being with Blue Flame you fill,
your power allows me to forge on until,
I pierce every veil and climb every hill.**

8. I establish oneness and co-create with my I AM Presence a positive response, an uplifting response, a response that seeks to raise the other person rather than defend myself or attack back and seek to tear the other person down.

O Hercules Blue, your Temple of Light,
revealed to us all through our inner sight,
a beacon that radiates light to the earth,
bringing about our planet's rebirth.

**O Hercules Blue, all life you defend,
giving us power to always transcend,
in you the expansion of self has no end,
as I in God's infinite spirals ascend.**

9. In any situation I encounter, I want to be *more* in that situation. I will not allow anything to force me to be less than the infinitely creative co-creator I am created to be. I choose to serve the *more*.

> Accelerate into Creativity, I AM real,
> Accelerate into Creativity, all life heal,
> Accelerate into Creativity, I AM MORE,
> Accelerate into Creativity, all will soar.

> Accelerate into Creativity! (3X)
> Beloved Hercules and Amazonia.
> Accelerate into Creativity! (3X)
> Beloved Michael and Faith.
> Accelerate into Creativity! (3X)
> Beloved Master MORE.
> Accelerate into Creativity! (3X)
> Beloved I AM.

4. I accept change in my life

1. I recognize the reality that all is an expression of consciousness and that all elements of consciousness are the result of choices I make. I accept that I am more than the identity that feels trapped in the material universe.

Master MORE, come to the fore,
I will absorb your flame of MORE.
Master MORE, my will so strong,
my power center cleared by song.

O Holy Spirit, flow through me,
I am the open door for thee.
O mighty rushing stream of Light,
transcendence is my sacred right.

2. I choose to be more than a human being, to be more than a preprogrammed biological robot. I choose to systematically resolve all attachments so that the prince of this world has nothing in me whereby he can control me.

Master MORE, your wisdom flows,
as my attunement ever grows.
Master MORE, we have a tie,
that helps me see through Serpent's lie.

O Holy Spirit, flow through me,
I am the open door for thee.
O mighty rushing stream of Light,
transcendence is my sacred right.

3. I choose to make creative choices. I choose to be *more* than the people who want me to fall back into the old patterns of less. I choose to be *more* and to express it.

> Master MORE, your love so pink,
> there is no purer love, I think.
> Master MORE, you set me free,
> from all conditionality.

> **O Holy Spirit, flow through me,**
> **I am the open door for thee.**
> **O mighty rushing stream of Light,**
> **transcendence is my sacred right.**

4. I accept that my mind is designed to be creative, and I cannot be satisfied by a life that has become a broken record. I tune in to my desire to move on and I free myself from these endless patterns of repetition.

> Master MORE, I will endure,
> your discipline that makes me pure.
> Master MORE, intentions true,
> as I am always one with you.

> **O Holy Spirit, flow through me,**
> **I am the open door for thee.**
> **O mighty rushing stream of Light,**
> **transcendence is my sacred right.**

5. I accept that I have the potential to rise to an entirely different level and to experience an absolute turning point in my personal life. I am making the choice to be *more* and I will reinforce it no matter what happens in my life.

Master MORE, my vision raised,
the will of God is always praised.
Master MORE, creative will,
raising all life higher still.

O Holy Spirit, flow through me,
I am the open door for thee.
O mighty rushing stream of Light,
transcendence is my sacred right.

6. I accept that I am at the point where I have the potential to permanently put myself beyond the downward pull of the collective consciousness. I am always choosing to be *more*, no matter what the situation might be.

Master MORE, your peace is power,
the demons of war it will devour.
Master MORE, we serve all life,
our flames consuming war and strife.

O Holy Spirit, flow through me,
I am the open door for thee.
O mighty rushing stream of Light,
transcendence is my sacred right.

7. I accept that I am at the point that people were at when Jesus walked up to them and said: "Leave your nets and follow me." I am ready to leave my nets and show people that there is indeed *more*.

Master MORE, I am so free,
eternal bond from you to me.
Master MORE, I find rebirth,
in flow of your eternal mirth.

O Holy Spirit, flow through me,
I am the open door for thee.
O mighty rushing stream of Light,
transcendence is my sacred right.

8. I now go within and reconnect to the moment where my very being chose to descend into this world to bring the light and the unconditional love of God. That is the choice—the spontaneous, completely unified, unconditional choice that nothing in this world can oppose.

Master MORE, you balance all,
the seven rays upon my call.
Master MORE, forever MORE,
I am the Spirit's open door.

O Holy Spirit, flow through me,
I am the open door for thee.
O mighty rushing stream of Light,
transcendence is my sacred right.

9. I choose from that level of my being, and it is a sustainable choice, a permanent choice. I will *be*, and I AM above anti-Being.

> Master MORE, your Presence here,
> filling up my inner sphere.
> Life is now a sacred flow,
> God Power I on all bestow.

> **O Holy Spirit, flow through me,**
> **I am the open door for thee.**
> **O mighty rushing stream of Light,**
> **transcendence is my sacred right.**

Sealing:

In the name of the Divine Mother, I fully accept that the power of these calls is used to set free the Ma-ter light, so it can outpicture the perfect vision of Christ for my own life, for all people and for the planet. In the name I AM THAT I AM, it is done! Amen.

4 | MORE THAN INTELLECTUAL KNOWLEDGE

A dictation by Elohim Apollo, representing the Second Ray of God's wisdom.

Apollo is my name, and I AM known as the Elohim of the Second Ray of God's wisdom. I come, then, to give you the perspective of communication from the heart and how it relates to the Second Ray of wisdom.

The challenge you face is being who you are in the midst of the non-being that is rampant on this planet. This non-being has ruled the planet for so long that the force behind it has come to believe that it owns this planet and is entitled to this ownership. It is not about to see a small band of people rise above its control and demonstrate to the world that they are willing to be unconditional love in the face of all conditions.

The misuse of religion

Even though it may be painful to face personal issues, you might recognize that if humankind is to grow and overcome the limitations they face, then some people must be willing to be the forerunners – to be that tip of the spear – and demonstrate that they are willing to deal with their personal issues so as to inspire others to do likewise.

What we have been saying – now in many different contexts and with many different wordings – is that for a very long time on this planet religion has been used as a tool by the false teachers in order to create the impression that you can enter the kingdom of God without looking at the beam in your own eye, without looking at the ego. There is an entire consciousness hanging as a dark cloud over this planet. Those who are actually the most spiritual people have become seduced by this belief that they can find some ultimate religion or guru that will then do all the work for them. Or they can find some magical formula that will enable them to enter the kingdom of God without going through the unpleasant work of looking at their egos and undoing their past choices by making a better choice, because they have come to see – even though it may be painful for a time – how their past choices are limiting them.

Only when you are willing to look at your past choices in that capacity, can you then recognize that you are *more* than the identity built through those past choices. You can rise above it, you can leave it behind, you can let it go into the fire of the Being that you are.

What the heart is full of

Master MORE has built a magnificent foundation by talking about the will of God in relation to communication from the heart. Truly, there are many people in this world who do not want to communicate from the heart, for they do not even want to connect to the oneness of the heart. In fact, one might go one step further and refer to the teachings of Christ who said that what the heart is full of, the mouth overflows with. The heart can, indeed, have certain colorings or shadings of negativity or anger.

This, of course, does not mean that the heart – understood as the core of your being – has taken on this negativity. The core of your being cannot be overpowered by anything on earth. It *does* mean that you can allow your heart chakra to be filled with a certain negative outlook and the vibrations that are associated with it. You can actually see people in the world where we might say that their hearts – meaning their fundamental outlook on life, their fundamental approach to life – has taken on a particular manifestation of anti-love.

By default they tend to react to life in a certain way by either responding with negativity or by projecting negativity upon others. That is what the mouth will overflow with when they are confronted with any situation that does not meet their expectations. Those expectations, of course, being entirely determined by the outlook on life that they have chosen to accept and which they see as the ultimate reality. They fail to see that it is simply an unreal illusion of the duality consciousness that they have chosen to accept as real and that they have chosen to project upon the Ma-ter light.

If the heart has been colored by such a negative manifestation, then these people are often unwilling to recognize that it is unreal, that it is the result of a choice they made. They will instead project the image that this is fully and wholly the way things are—because they live in a parallel universe that is dominated by fear, anger, or whatever manifestation they have chosen as their basic approach to life.

Look at your own heart

You who are the wise ones have started purifying your hearts. You have started rising above it, but some of you still have certain elements of anti-love in your heart chakras that then color how you look at life. What I endeavor to help you understand here is that the light from your I AM Presence first enters your being in the secret chamber of the heart and then enters the heart chakra. You might see that when there is an element of unreality in your heart chakra, it will color the light in its first manifestation in your lower being. That is indeed why those elements of unreality in your heart chakra can be extremely difficult to see through—for you have come to believe that this is simply the way things are.

You are reluctant to step back and say: "Could this possibly be an illusion?" You think – often – that you simply do not have to ask that question. You think that whereas you might have gone through many other breakthroughs in your psychology, whereas you might have overcome other attachments or given up other illusions, this particular element of your being does not need to be questioned. It is indeed based on reality, the reality that you think it has because it is infused with the light that comes from your I AM Presence. You see the force of the light, but you do not see that the light has been colored by that particular dualistic illusion that you have accepted as reality.

How can you come to see through these core illusions? Well, only by encountering a living guru. With a living guru I do not mean a person who has some kind of stature or education or some kind of authority. I mean that you encounter the living guru in one of its many disguises. Did not Master MORE say: "If the guru be an ant, heed him?" Do you not all know the old fairy tale of the emperor's new clothes where it was the little child who cried out: "But the emperor has nothing on?"

Humility is an essential ingredient on the path

The question is: "Are you willing to let your peers tell you that there is something you do not see?" Are you willing to see that there is some element of unreality that has entered so close to the core of your lower being that you do not see it as unreality or do not believe you need to question it?

If the spiritual seekers are to fulfill their ultimate potential, then we need to have people who are willing to, so to speak, air their dirty laundry in public and demonstrate that they are willing to look at anything in their psychology and then overcome it and leave it behind. This is, indeed, what will inspire humankind to come up higher. This is what will help them see that the old illusion of the automatic salvation without looking at the beam in your own eye is simply an unreality. It is a lie, a false path to salvation that is meant to take them off the true path demonstrated by Christ, the Buddha, by Lao Tzu and any other spiritual teacher that has truly been connected and understood the oneness of all life.

Receiving from the heart

When you have that willingness to let other people tell you what you do not see, then you need to take the next step. You need to realize that the only way you can come to see what you do not currently see is to go beyond the outer mind and allow people to communicate to you from their hearts—but you also receive it from your heart. Communication is a two-way process, is it not? Or at least it is meant to be, if it is to be successful.

I can tell you that communication from the heart cannot truly occur unless there is the Alpha-to-Omega flow of giving and receiving. Another person may be seeking to tell you something and may truly be connected and speaking from the heart, but if you are not willing to connect to the heart and receive from the heart, then the communication will not have the effect of helping you see what you do not see. You cannot come up higher. You will instead go into the lower, fear-based reaction of defending what you cannot see, defending the illusion that you believe is reality.

This, of course, is what you see going on in the world over and over again where people go into the reaction of defending their illusions, arguing why they are reality or why they do not need to question them. Perhaps they even go to the extreme of attacking those that they think are attacking themselves or attacking their illusion—their world view, their cherished religion or political ideology.

Be wiser than the ego

You need to be wiser. You need to use that wisdom of the Second Ray and say: "I will be *more* than the people who defend their illusions. I will indeed enter into the heart. I will not go into the analytical mind and seek to defend my illusion when someone comes to tell me something from the heart."

Sometimes there will be people who are trying to tell you something about yourself and they will not be entirely centered in the heart. They may have a certain vibration of frustration or anger because after having put up with you for some time, they have finally gotten fed up and now they are speaking out. This is one of the most common reasons why people find an excuse for not listening to others. But I tell you that if you are the wise ones, then you will say that whenever someone says something to you, you will look beyond the imperfections of the other person. You will look beyond the vibration. You will look beyond the words. You will go within your heart and say: "Is there something here that is real, that I need to see? Does this person have a point? Has this person seen, even if imperfectly, something in me that needs to be corrected?"

You must, of course, also be wise to another entrapment of the ego, namely the tendency to use the analytical mind to argue for or against your beliefs, to argue for and against what the other person is saying. You must become wise and use the teachings we have given on the duality consciousness [See the books *Freedom From Ego Illusions*, *Freedom From Ego Games* and *Freedom From Ego Dramas*] and realize that the duality consciousness can prove any point. For the duality consciousness is based on the analytical faculty of the mind, the intellect.

Know the limitations of the intellect

It is not my intention to say here that the intellect is a bad thing and is something you should avoid. The intellect is simply a necessary part of the mind. But it is a part of the mind that is specifically designed to help you deal with the world of form. As we have explained – most profoundly by Mother Mary and Maitreya in their books – the world of form is characterized by differences, which is what makes one form stand out compared to another. The analytical mind is simply designed to help you deal with these differences, analyzing and categorizing the various characteristics that separate one form from another. It even allows you to make some judgments about what is constructive and what is non-constructive, what actually expands yourself and all life or what restricts yourself and restricts all life.

This can, to some degree, be done by the intellect, especially when the intellect is under the tutelage of the heart. Of course, as with any other faculty, the intellect can become an end in itself. You see those who are never connected to the heart and who believe that the intellect is superior and has no need to be under the tutelage of the heart, for it is perfectly capable of knowing truth on its own. As I said, the intellect is designed to help you distinguish between what is in the world of form. The intellect cannot discover ultimate truth, ultimate reality. It cannot even deal with these concepts.

You see many people who have been trapped by the intellect and who will argue for hours for a particular world view or idea, although they actually realize that on a deeper level they do not believe there is any ultimate truth or any ultimate argument. After all, they see that any argument with the intellect can always be counteracted with another argument, and they have come to believe that there is no ultimate truth.

Knowing ultimate truth

How will you connect to ultimate truth? Well, only through the heart, my beloved. Only the heart, as Master MORE has said, can connect to the ultimate reality that all life is one. This realization is, of course, the ultimate expression of wisdom. You will see that there is intellectual knowledge, which is very good at coming up with all the details but is not very good at seeing the big picture—for only the heart can see the big picture. Naturally, the intellect – being focused on differences, being designed to analyze and categorize differences – cannot reveal, cannot fathom, the underlying reality of the oneness of all life.

Those who are trapped in the intellect are trapped in seeing themselves separated from others, separated from God. Suddenly, the existence of God and the nature of God becomes a topic for intellectual argumentation. Rather than being seen as a challenge to connect to that God, to experience God directly in the heart, rather than arguing which image of the remote, external God is the ultimate one. This is what many intellectual theologians have done over the ages, of course, without ever coming one step closer to the direct experience of the oneness of God's Being.

Transcending expectations

The question really is: "Do you want to connect to other people in the heart?" The answer will determine the level of wisdom of whether you still see yourself as separated from them or whether you see, or at least begin to see, that underlying reality of all life. Are you seeking to raise up the separate self? Are you seeking to defend the separate self? Are you seeking to avoid being hurt? Or are you in all situations seeking to raise up all life?

I encourage you to read Master More's words many times over, for there are indeed hidden keys that hardly any one of you will get on the first encounter. I encourage you to meditate on his words with the heart until you recognize the underlying reality. When you truly experience the reality and the wisdom of free will, you know that there is no point – there is no justification – in having any expectation about how things should or should not be on earth.

When you have wisdom, you realize that this statement does not mean that you go through life uncritically accepting everything the way it is. Truly, how would things ever change unless there are those who have a drive for the *more*, the drive to transcend what is manifest right now? You recognize that you are not going to affect change on earth by having this standard and then comparing other people and their actions to that standard—judging them with a human judgment and saying that they are wrong for not living up to that standard. The fallen beings are seeking to change the earth, and some of them believe they are seeking to save humankind through control, through forcing people to act in certain ways. They think that if people live up to this outer standard, they will be allowed into the kingdom of God.

Inspiration instead of force

The reality is, of course, that there is only one way to enter the kingdom of God, and that is to realize that you were never separated from it—for the kingdom of God is all that is. The only way to affect positive change on earth is not through force, but through inspiration—through inspiring other people to make better choices.

Those who have set themselves up as the false teachers have separated themselves from the oneness of all life. As a result of that, they are seeking to control and force other people by overriding their free will. Only through free-will choices can you enter the kingdom of God, can you choose to be in that kingdom as opposed to choosing not to be in that kingdom. You cannot force other people to make that choice, my beloved. You can force other people to perform certain actions, you can even force other people to accept certain beliefs. But you cannot force people to *be*. This must come as the result of a free-will choice from within that being.

If you think that you are working for the light, working for the ascended masters, working for the upliftment of all mankind, yet you have this subtle sense that you have to force people to accept certain beliefs – perhaps even forcing them to come into a certain religion – well then, you are actually not working for the light, you are working against the light.

This is the case for many truly well-meaning people in the religious world who have become trapped in this illusion of the automatic, external salvation. You, who are the wise ones, must free your hearts from all elements of this illusion so that you do not seek to force others. Instead, you seek to inspire them to make better choices.

Why is the world the way it is?

Why is the world the way it is? As a result of the collective choices – or rather the individual choices forming a collective whole – that have created these conditions. How will they change? Only when a critical mass of individuals change their previous choices by realizing the wisdom of making a better choice.

You cannot force them to see that wisdom. You can only inspire them by teaching—but how do you really teach? You teach by demonstrating, by *being*, by being one with that wisdom. You teach by demonstrating that you have been willing to look at the illusions, both in the world around you – which is somewhat safe and easy, for after all, it is someone else who has created those illusions – but also by looking at the illusions in your own being. You realize that even though you may have accepted certain illusions externally, you have also created certain illusions yourself.

Why do you create certain illusions? Well, you create them so that you have a justification for not being *more*, a justification for withholding your light. Truly, you came into this world to be a Sun and to radiate your particular shade of God's unconditional love. When your love was rejected over and over by those who have forgotten that they are children of love, you decided to start withholding your light from the profane. You had to justify why it was necessary or appropriate to withhold that light. In order to do that, you had to create certain illusions that have then entered into the core of your lower being, your heart chakra, and thus color the very way you look at the world and even look at yourself.

Resistance to giving

If you have any reluctance in your being towards giving – and I mean giving freely and unconditionally – then you have created an illusion that justifies why you are not giving, why you do not have to give, why you should not give, why it is impossible to give, why it is improper to give. There are innumerable such illusions, but they are precisely that: illusions, my beloved.

You did not come here to withhold your light. You came here because you saw that the reason why this planet is in darkness is that the majority of the people on it are withholding their light. You came to make a difference!

You will not make a difference by doing what everybody else is doing—withholding your light. This I trust you can see.

How will you make a difference? By doing something that other people are not doing. By giving unconditionally, which does not mean giving stupidly, but giving with wisdom. You are not giving your light and energy to another in sympathy, in order to enable that person to stay in a limited state of consciousness. You are giving to raise another up beyond his or her present state of consciousness.

There are indeed certain situations where it might seem like you are withholding your light in order to avoid enabling another person. When you step back and look at this with greater wisdom, you realize that you are not actually withholding. It is just that you are directing, you are giving in such a way that it has the greatest opportunity for raising the other person up by inspiring that person to see that there is more to life. There are, indeed, situations where you do not go down to another person's level and state of consciousness and empathize with them, but where you actually give them your light by demonstrating that you are in a higher state of consciousness. You will not go down to their level of consciousness, you will stay clear of it—even if they are trying to pull you down so that they can have an excuse for not changing.

Giving with wisdom

There is a subtle difference here, which I endeavor to help you see, between withholding and giving with wisdom. Withholding means that you stop the flow. Giving with wisdom means that you redirect the flow in such a way as to affect the greatest possible result.

How can you know how to redirect that flow? Well, you cannot know it through the outer, analytical mind. You can know it through connecting to the heart and letting your own higher being direct that light through you. This is the control of the light, my beloved.

You do not seek to control others, which is what people do when they are in fear. You seek to always have control, God control, over your own state of mind so that you can, in any situation, choose not to respond with a preprogrammed response, as Master MORE said. You can choose to connect to the heart and therefore respond with a higher response, a response aimed at raising the other person up, even by confronting that person with the need to change, if necessary. You are – again – not judging this with the outer mind.

There are subtle ways to judge and therefore shut off the flow. Sometimes you may think: "This person has to change and they have to see it right now and I have to be tough on them." Other times you may think: "Oh, that person is upset. I cannot possibly be tough on them. I cannot tell them the truth. I need to step back and not demonstrate that I AM in a higher state of consciousness." You see – again – in duality there are always the two opposite polarities and even the unreality of the gray thinking in the middle. You must be wise to this and step back.

Again, you do not have to analyze. You need to connect to the heart and then let your higher being express itself through you.

The Sun is more than physical

The physical Sun that you see in the sky is not actually a material phenomenon. If these intellectual scientists who believe they know everything – or at least know that there is nothing beyond the material universe – if they were to use their science to measure the total output of energy from the physical Sun and then measure the internal processes that are going on in that Sun, they would see that there is actually a deficit between the two. The actual energy produced by the material processes of the Sun itself cannot account for the output of energy from the Sun. The physical Sun is simply an open door for the light from the spiritual realm to stream into the material world.

You are meant to also be such an open door. You may direct the light coming from your I AM Presence, but do not fall into the trap of directing it with the outer, analytical mind that so easily falls into human judgment. Instead, focus on lifting up all life rather than judging whether another person should do this or that.

Let the light flow, but observe how the light flows. Observe yourself. "Am I non-attached? Did I have some subtle judgment of that other person that may have prevented the light from being expressed through me to its highest potential?" Then gradually become wise where you rise above the intelligence of the intellect and even the intelligence of the false teachers who have infused every aspect of life on earth with their "sophisticated" dualistic reasonings. Rise above that—what some call wisdom. Then become wise to the wisdom of the heart, the wisdom that flows from your higher being and that your outer mind can grasp, or rather the Conscious You can grasp, for it is not truly the outer mind of the intellect that can grasp that wisdom.

Your database

Many times people trapped in the lower mind can come up with what they think are unassailable arguments for this or that or the next thing. This is what you will see, for example, outpictured in the scribes and the Pharisees, who challenged Christ, and in the Brahmins who challenged the Buddha. The one who has gone into the heart and connected to the oneness of all life can come up with a statement or a saying that confounds all of the best intellects on this planet, that jolts the mind. Therefore, it opens the heart to a direct experience that is beyond anything that can be analyzed and categorized by the intellect.

It is helpful when you are in physical embodiment to have a database where everything is categorized so that you can quickly respond to certain situations. When that database becomes an end in itself – and you think it contains all the wisdom you need – you do not step back and say: "Can I now compare my responses to the wisdom of my higher self and therefore gradually ascend to a higher response, one that is based on oneness, the oneness of all life and the desire of life itself to raise up all life, to raise the All?" This is the true wisdom of the ages.

Many spiritual people are very close to manifesting that kind of wisdom, many already having it in glimpses. But all of you could stand to focus on locking in to it and truly opening your minds and hearts to that higher wisdom, also allowing that higher wisdom – and allowing each other – to show you where you are still holding on to certain dualistic arguments and illusions that cause you to make subtle judgments about other people or about life on earth—what it should or should not be.

When you judge what life should be or should not be, you will also be judging yourself. When you are judging what you should be or should not be, well then, you cannot *be*. In analyzing something, you have separated yourself from it, and therefore you are not being. You cannot, as Master MORE said, be who you will be at any given moment, for you are now judging based on the idea that there is some predefined response to every situation.

Stop killing your creativity

Where is creativity, if everything is predefined? Again, my beloved, nothing is static in the reality of God. There are many spiritual teachings on this planet that cater to the subtle belief that there are certain invariable laws of God, and once you understand those laws and make use of them, then your salvation is guaranteed. Again – as we have said now in many different contexts and disguises – salvation is a creative process, not a mechanical one.

You might think about God Wisdom and think that up here in the spiritual realm we have a great book, and in that book is written all the wisdom of the world and it can never change. Wisdom is a creative force, and creativity is not predefined. It is indeed spontaneous.

There are many expressions of wisdom that we, who are the guardians of the Second Ray of God Wisdom, do not know because no one in the lower spheres has as yet chosen to express them—and thus surprise us to where we can say: "Well done thou good and faithful servant. Thou hast been faithful over a few things. I will make thee ruler over many things by giving you greater wisdom, for you have been willing to express that wisdom in new, creative, and surprising ways."

The "untouchable" within you

Be willing to let others tell you what you cannot see, and you will find that you will make much greater progress. It is a common reaction that you have a need to defend some aspect of your lower being as being untouchable, as being beyond criticism, as being beyond questioning.

There are some people who have gone beyond that point. They have gone beyond that fear of looking at something where they are willing to look at anything and everything, even expose it in public. When you are not seeking to protect the lower self, then why do you need to fear the exposure of it—if that exposure of some element of your lower self could inspire and help another. Well, is that not why you are here—ultimately?

Consider and observe that there are some among you who are free to speak about themselves and their own imperfections. There are others who never say anything. There are others who are somewhere in between. Consider that you all have the potential to be inspired by each other, to come to that point where there is nothing you need to defend, nothing you need to hide. If there is some element of duality in your consciousness, well then, your attitude is: "Let it be brought out in the open so I can see it, for I know I AM more than this. I want to see it so that I can rise above it and be freer than I was before."

Do you not see that those who have no fear are free? Even though they may still have certain manifestations of unreality they are dealing with, they are not so identified with it that they seek to protect or hide it. This is freedom. It is not yet the total freedom from duality, but it is the freedom of not being fully identified with duality and thus, knowing you are *more*.

Your God-given right to make better choices

Learn from that. Be inspired by it. Be inspired by the examples of spiritual teachers who have also come to that point. Do not focus on those who have been idolized by so many of their followers. Instead, look at the people who are just like you who have manifested a greater degree of freedom and say: "Well, I, too, want to be free. I want to be free so that I have no fear of any aspect of my lower self, any aspect of duality, being exposed. I know that whatever is exposed that I can see, I can then let go of and transcend. I have the God-given right that no matter what choices I have made in the past, I can make better choices in the present."

This is the right that the false teachers will deny you. Do not let them get away with this, for you have allowed them to get away with it for far too long. It is time now to break through, to take that stand, and let this book be a turning point in your life—and not just another inspirational reading where you do not actually look in the mirror and say: "Ah, this is where I need to change. This is unreality, and thus it is not part of me. I AM rising above it. I AM letting it go into the flame."

A new type of spiritual movement

Let me give you a realistic assessment of your potential. You may look at yourselves, you may look at your limited numbers, you may look at your imperfections, but I can tell you that many among today's spiritual seekers have the willingness to look at their psychology, to look at the ego, and they have demonstrated it many times over.

You have, indeed, the potential to form a movement where the ego cannot hide, the ego cannot play its games. You are willing to expose it and confront it, and thus you have the potential to set an example for what a spiritual movement should be in the Aquarian Age, indeed what a spiritual movement *must* be if the Aquarian Age is to become the Golden Age of Saint Germain. This can only happen when the ego is exposed so that it cannot stay in hiding and play its games that can only be played when they are not seen for what they are. For this we congratulate you, we encourage you, we inspire you to come up higher, to go further. With that, my beloved, I bless you with the Second Ray of God Wisdom, and I seal you in the unconditional wisdom that I AM.

I leave you with this last koan that you might, indeed, ponder unconditional wisdom and what it truly is and ponder how it relates to unconditional love. Ponder, indeed, how unconditionality can still have shadings of wisdom, love, will, power, purity, truth, healing, service, freedom, and all of these God qualities and yet avoid falling into the trap of separation, the trap of opposition, but still remaining one. In pondering this, you will see how you yourselves can remain individuals but still come into unity and form that community of the Holy Spirit. Community: "come ye into unity." Communication: "come ye into unity and then take action from that unity." This is your potential. *Be it to the fullest!*

5 | I INVOKE
UNCONDITIONAL WISDOM

In the name I AM THAT I AM, Jesus Christ, I call to my I AM Presence to flow through the I Will Be Presence that I AM and give this invocation with full power. I call to beloved Elohim Apollo and Lumina, Archangel Jophiel and Christine, and Lord Lanto to help me overcome all blocks to my wisdom to communicate from the heart in all situations. Help me be free from all patterns or forces within or without that oppose my communication from the heart and my oneness with my I AM Presence, including ...

[Make personal calls]

I. I am willing to see unreality

1. I am willing to be among the forerunners. I demonstrate that I am willing to deal with my personal issues and inspire others to do likewise.

Beloved Apollo, with your Second Ray,
you open my eyes to see a new day,
I see through duality's lies and deceit,
transcending the mindset producing defeat.

Beloved Apollo, thou Elohim Gold,
your radiant light my eyes now behold,
as pages of wisdom you gently unfold,
I feel I am free from all that is old.

2. I am willing to do the work of looking at my ego and undoing my past choices by making better choices. I see that I am *more* than the identity built through past choices. I rise above it and let it go into the fire of the Being that I AM.

Beloved Apollo, in your flame I know,
that your living wisdom is always a flow,
in your light I see my own highest will,
immersed in the stream that never stands still.

Beloved Apollo, your light makes it clear,
why we have taken embodiment here,
working to raise our own cosmic sphere,
together we form the tip of the spear.

3. I AM purifying my heart chakra from any negative outlook and the vibrations of fear and anger. I am surrendering all expectations based on anti-love for I know they are only the illusions of duality.

Beloved Apollo, exposing all lies,
I hereby surrender all ego-based ties,
I know my perception is truly the key,
to transcending the serpentine duality.

**Beloved Apollo, we heed now your call,
drawing us into Wisdom's Great Hall,
exposing all lies causing the fall,
you help us reclaim the oneness of all.**

4. I am transcending any element of unreality in my heart chakra that colors the light from my I AM Presence. I am willing to let the Living Guru expose any illusion that I have accepted as reality.

Beloved Apollo, your wisdom so clear,
in oneness with you, no serpent I fear,
the beam in my eye I'm willing to see,
I'm free from the serpent's own duality.

**Beloved Apollo, my eyes now I raise,
I see that the earth is in a new phase,
I willingly stand in your piercing gaze,
empowered, I exit duality's maze.**

5. I am willing to let my peers show me what I do not see. I am willing to see any element of unreality that has entered so close to the core of my lower being that I do not see it as unreality or do not believe I need to question it.

> Beloved Apollo, with your Second Ray,
> you open my eyes to see a new day,
> I see through duality's lies and deceit,
> transcending the mindset producing defeat.

> **Beloved Apollo, thou Elohim Gold,**
> **your radiant light my eyes now behold,**
> **as pages of wisdom you gently unfold,**
> **I feel I am free from all that is old.**

6. I am willing to look at anything in my psychology and over-come it and leave it behind. I will help inspire humankind to let go of the old illusion of the automatic salvation. I will walk the true path demonstrated by Christ, the Buddha, by Lao Tzu and other spiritual teachers.

> Beloved Apollo, in your flame I know,
> that your living wisdom is always a flow,
> in your light I see my own highest will,
> immersed in the stream that never stands still.

> **Beloved Apollo, your light makes it clear,**
> **why we have taken embodiment here,**
> **working to raise our own cosmic sphere,**
> **together we form the tip of the spear.**

7. I am willing to go beyond the outer mind and allow people to communicate to me from their hearts. I will receive what they say from my heart and enter the Alpha-to-Omega flow of giving and receiving.

> Beloved Apollo, exposing all lies,
> I hereby surrender all ego-based ties,
> I know my perception is truly the key,
> to transcending the serpentine duality.

> **Beloved Apollo, we heed now your call,**
> **drawing us into Wisdom's Great Hall,**
> **exposing all lies causing the fall,**
> **you help us reclaim the oneness of all.**

8. I will use the wisdom of the Second Ray and I say: "I will be *more* than the people who defend their illusions. I will enter into the heart. I will not go into the analytical mind and seek to defend my illusion when someone comes to tell me something from the heart."

> Beloved Apollo, your wisdom so clear,
> in oneness with you, no serpent I fear,
> the beam in my eye I'm willing to see,
> I'm free from the serpent's own duality.

> **Beloved Apollo, my eyes now I raise,**
> **I see that the earth is in a new phase,**
> **I willingly stand in your piercing gaze,**
> **empowered, I exit duality's maze.**

9. I will look beyond the imperfections of other people and go within my heart and say: "Is there something here that is real, that I need to see? Does this person have a point? Has this person seen, even if imperfectly, something in me that needs to be transcended?"

> Accelerate my Awakeness, I AM real,
> Accelerate my Awakeness, all life heal,
> Accelerate my Awakeness, I AM MORE,
> Accelerate my Awakeness, all will soar.
>
> Accelerate my Awakeness! (3X)
> Beloved Apollo and Lumina.
> Accelerate my Awakeness! (3X)
> Beloved Jophiel and Christine.
> Accelerate my Awakeness! (3X)
> Beloved Master Lanto.
> Accelerate my Awakeness! (3X)
> Beloved I AM.

2. I am willing to connect in my heart

1. I am willing to have my I AM Presence show me the way beyond the dualistic reasoning of the intellect. I accept that the intellect must be under the tutelage of the heart.

> Jophiel Archangel, in wisdom's great light,
> all serpentine lies exposed to my sight.
> So subtle the lies that creep through the mind,
> yet you are the greatest teacher I find.

> **Jophiel Archangel, exposing all lies,**
> **Jophiel Archangel, cutting all ties.**
> **Jophiel Archangel, clearing the skies,**
> **Jophiel Archangel, my mind truly flies.**

2. I see that the intellect cannot discover ultimate truth, ultimate reality. I am willing to connect to ultimate truth through the heart. I am willing to connect to the ultimate wisdom that all life is one.

> Jophiel Archangel, your wisdom I hail,
> your sword cutting through duality's veil.
> As you show the way, I know what is real,
> from serpentine doubt, I instantly heal.

> **Jophiel Archangel, exposing all lies,**
> **Jophiel Archangel, cutting all ties.**
> **Jophiel Archangel, clearing the skies,**
> **Jophiel Archangel, my mind truly flies.**

3. I will not allow the intellect to trap me in seeing myself separated from others, separated from God. I am willing to connect to my God, to experience God directly in my heart, surrendering all images of the remote, external God.

> Jophiel Archangel, your reality,
> the best antidote to duality.
> No lie can remain in your Presence so clear,
> with you on my side, no serpent I fear.

Jophiel Archangel, exposing all lies,
Jophiel Archangel, cutting all ties.
Jophiel Archangel, clearing the skies,
Jophiel Archangel, my mind truly flies.

4. I am willing to connect to other people in my heart. I want the level of wisdom where I do not see myself separated from others but see the underlying oneness of all life. In all situations I am seeking to raise up all life.

> Jophiel Archangel, God's mind is in me,
> and through your clear light, its wisdom I see.
> Divisions all vanish, as I see the One,
> and truly, the wholeness of mind I have won.

Jophiel Archangel, exposing all lies,
Jophiel Archangel, cutting all ties.
Jophiel Archangel, clearing the skies,
Jophiel Archangel, my mind truly flies.

5. I experience the reality and the wisdom of free will. I surrender any expectation about how things should or should not be on earth. I am an instrument for change because I have a drive to transcend what is manifest right now.

Jophiel Archangel, in wisdom's great light,
all serpentine lies exposed to my sight.
So subtle the lies that creep through the mind,
yet you are the greatest teacher I find.

Jophiel Archangel, exposing all lies,
Jophiel Archangel, cutting all ties.
Jophiel Archangel, clearing the skies,
Jophiel Archangel, my mind truly flies.

6. I recognize that I am not going to affect change on earth by having a standard and then comparing other people to that standard. I surrender my human standard and all judgments based on that dualistic standard.

Jophiel Archangel, your wisdom I hail,
your sword cutting through duality's veil.
As you show the way, I know what is real,
from serpentine doubt, I instantly heal.

Jophiel Archangel, exposing all lies,
Jophiel Archangel, cutting all ties.
Jophiel Archangel, clearing the skies,
Jophiel Archangel, my mind truly flies.

7. I see that there is only one way to enter the kingdom of God, and that is to realize that I was never separated from it—for the kingdom of God is all that is.

> Jophiel Archangel, your reality,
> the best antidote to duality.
> No lie can remain in your Presence so clear,
> with you on my side, no serpent I fear.

> **Jophiel Archangel, exposing all lies,**
> **Jophiel Archangel, cutting all ties.**
> **Jophiel Archangel, clearing the skies,**
> **Jophiel Archangel, my mind truly flies.**

8. I see that the way to affect positive change on earth is not through force, but through inspiration—through inspiring other people to make better choices.

> Jophiel Archangel, God's mind is in me,
> and through your clear light, its wisdom I see.
> Divisions all vanish, as I see the One,
> and truly, the wholeness of mind I have won.

> **Jophiel Archangel, exposing all lies,**
> **Jophiel Archangel, cutting all ties.**
> **Jophiel Archangel, clearing the skies,**
> **Jophiel Archangel, my mind truly flies.**

9. I see and accept that only through free-will choices can we enter the kingdom of God. I choose to be in that kingdom as opposed to choosing not to be in that kingdom.

> With angels I soar,
> as I reach for MORE.
> The angels so real,
> their love all will heal.
> The angels bring peace,
> all conflicts will cease.
> With angels of light,
> we soar to new height.

> **The rustling sound of angel wings,**
> **what joy as even matter sings,**
> **what joy as every atom rings,**
> **in harmony with angel wings.**

3. I will let my light shine

1. I surrender all subtle sense that I have to force other people to make certain choices. I free my heart from all elements of this illusion. I do not seek to force others. I seek to inspire them to make better choices.

> Beloved Apollo, with your Second Ray,
> you open my eyes to see a new day,
> I see through duality's lies and deceit,
> transcending the mindset producing defeat.

> **Beloved Apollo, thou Elohim Gold,**
> **your radiant light my eyes now behold,**
> **as pages of wisdom you gently unfold,**
> **I feel I am free from all that is old.**

2. I surrender all desires to force people to accept the wisdom of the Second Ray. I seek to inspire people by demonstrating, by *being*, by being one with that wisdom.

> Beloved Apollo, in your flame I know,
> that your living wisdom is always a flow,
> in your light I see my own highest will,
> immersed in the stream that never stands still.

> **Beloved Apollo, your light makes it clear,**
> **why we have taken embodiment here,**
> **working to raise our own cosmic sphere,**
> **together we form the tip of the spear.**

3. I am willing to look at the illusions I have accepted externally and those I have created internally. I am willing to see the illusions I have created as a justification for not being *more*, a justification for withholding my light.

> Beloved Apollo, exposing all lies,
> I hereby surrender all ego-based ties,
> I know my perception is truly the key,
> to transcending the serpentine duality.

> **Beloved Apollo, we heed now your call,**
> **drawing us into Wisdom's Great Hall,**
> **exposing all lies causing the fall,**
> **you help us reclaim the oneness of all.**

4. I came into this world to be a Sun and to radiate my particular shade of God's unconditional love. When my love was rejected, I decided to start withholding my light. I justified this by creating certain illusions that have entered my heart chakra and color the way I look at everything.

> Beloved Apollo, your wisdom so clear,
> in oneness with you, no serpent I fear,
> the beam in my eye I'm willing to see,
> I'm free from the serpent's own duality.

> **Beloved Apollo, my eyes now I raise,**
> **I see that the earth is in a new phase,**
> **I willingly stand in your piercing gaze,**
> **empowered, I exit duality's maze.**

5. I surrender all illusions that justify why I am not giving, why I do not have to give, why I should not give, why it is impossible to give, why it is improper to give. I am back in the innocence of giving freely and unconditionally.

Beloved Apollo, with your Second Ray,
you open my eyes to see a new day,
I see through duality's lies and deceit,
transcending the mindset producing defeat.

**Beloved Apollo, thou Elohim Gold,
your radiant light my eyes now behold,
as pages of wisdom you gently unfold,
I feel I am free from all that is old.**

6. I did not come here to withhold my light. I saw that this planet is in darkness because most people are withholding their light. I came to make a difference by freely letting my light shine.

Beloved Apollo, in your flame I know,
that your living wisdom is always a flow,
in your light I see my own highest will,
immersed in the stream that never stands still.

**Beloved Apollo, your light makes it clear,
why we have taken embodiment here,
working to raise our own cosmic sphere,
together we form the tip of the spear.**

7. I am giving unconditionally, yet I am giving with wisdom. I am in the flow of giving, and I am directing the flow in order to affect the greatest possible result of raising up others.

Beloved Apollo, exposing all lies,
I hereby surrender all ego-based ties,
I know my perception is truly the key,
to transcending the serpentine duality.

**Beloved Apollo, we heed now your call,
drawing us into Wisdom's Great Hall,
exposing all lies causing the fall,
you help us reclaim the oneness of all.**

8. I am giving by connecting to the heart and letting my I AM Presence direct the light flowing through me. I have God control over my own state of mind. In any situation, I choose to connect to the heart and find a higher response. I seek to raise up other people, even by confronting them with the need to change.

Beloved Apollo, your wisdom so clear,
in oneness with you, no serpent I fear,
the beam in my eye I'm willing to see,
I'm free from the serpent's own duality.

**Beloved Apollo, my eyes now I raise,
I see that the earth is in a new phase,
I willingly stand in your piercing gaze,
empowered, I exit duality's maze.**

9. I am an open door and I direct the light from my I AM Presence. I let the light flow, and I observe how the light flows. I am nonattached because I have the wisdom of the heart, the wisdom that flows from my I AM Presence.

Accelerate my Awakeness, I AM real,
Accelerate my Awakeness, all life heal,
Accelerate my Awakeness, I AM MORE,
Accelerate my Awakeness, all will soar.

Accelerate my Awakeness! (3X)
Beloved Apollo and Lumina.
Accelerate my Awakeness! (3X)
Beloved Jophiel and Christine.
Accelerate my Awakeness! (3X)
Beloved Master Lanto.
Accelerate my Awakeness! (3X)
Beloved I AM.

4. I seek higher wisdom

1. I am the open door for statements that confound the intellect, that jolt the mind. My I AM Presence opens the heart to a direct experience that is beyond anything that can be analyzed and categorized by the intellect.

> Master Lanto, golden wise,
> expose in me the ego's lies.
> Master Lanto, will to be,
> I will to win my mastery.

**O Holy Spirit, flow through me,
I am the open door for thee.
O mighty rushing stream of Light,
transcendence is my sacred right.**

2. I am constantly refining my personal database. I am evaluating my responses through the wisdom of my I AM Presence, the wisdom of the ages. I am ascending to a higher response based on oneness, the oneness of all life and the desire of life itself to raise up the All.

> Master Lanto, balance all,
> for wisdom's balance I do call.
> Master Lanto, help me see,
> that balance is the Golden key.

**O Holy Spirit, flow through me,
I am the open door for thee.
O mighty rushing stream of Light,
transcendence is my sacred right.**

3. I am locking in to the higher wisdom, opening my mind and heart to it. I am allowing that higher wisdom to show me where I am still holding on to certain dualistic arguments and illusions. I surrender all subtle judgments about other people or about life on earth—what it should or should not be.

> Master Lanto, from Above,
> I call forth discerning love.
> Master Lanto, love's not blind,
> through love, God vision I will find.

> **O Holy Spirit, flow through me,**
> **I am the open door for thee.**
> **O mighty rushing stream of Light,**
> **transcendence is my sacred right.**

4. I surrender all tendency to judge myself. I see that when I am judging what I should be or should not be, then I cannot BE. In analyzing something, I have separated myself from it, and therefore I am not being.

> Master Lanto, pure I am,
> intentions pure as Christic lamb.
> Master Lanto, I will transcend,
> acceleration now my truest friend.

> **O Holy Spirit, flow through me,**
> **I am the open door for thee.**
> **O mighty rushing stream of Light,**
> **transcendence is my sacred right.**

5. I am willing to express wisdom in new, creative, and surprising ways, so that the masters of wisdom can say: "Well done thou good and faithful servant. Thou hast been faithful over a few things. I will make thee ruler over many things by giving you greater wisdom."

Master Lanto, I am whole,
no more division in my soul.
Master Lanto, healing flame,
all balance in your sacred name.

**O Holy Spirit, flow through me,
I am the open door for thee.
O mighty rushing stream of Light,
transcendence is my sacred right.**

6. I surrender the need to defend some aspect of my lower being as untouchable. I surrender all fear of looking at something in myself. I am willing to look at anything and everything.

Master Lanto, serve all life,
as I transcend all inner strife.
Master Lanto, peace you give,
to all who want to truly live.

**O Holy Spirit, flow through me,
I am the open door for thee.
O mighty rushing stream of Light,
transcendence is my sacred right.**

7. I am willing to come to the point where there is nothing I need to defend, nothing I need to hide. If there is some element of duality in my consciousness, I say: "Let it be brought out in the open so I can see it, for I know I AM *more* than this. I want to see it so that I can rise above it and be freer than I was before."

Master Lanto, free to be,
in balanced creativity.
Master Lanto, we employ,
your balance as the key to joy.

O Holy Spirit, flow through me,
I am the open door for thee.
O mighty rushing stream of Light,
transcendence is my sacred right.

8. I am inspired by the examples of spiritual teachers, and thus I say: "I, too, want to be free so that I have no fear of any aspect of my lower self, any aspect of duality, being exposed. I know that whatever is exposed, I can let go of and transcend. No matter what choices I have made in the past, I can make better choices in the present."

Master Lanto, balance all,
the seven rays upon my call.
Master Lanto, I take flight,
my threefold flame a blazing light.

O Holy Spirit, flow through me,
I am the open door for thee.
O mighty rushing stream of Light,
transcendence is my sacred right.

9. I accept my right to transcend anything from the past. I accept that this is a turning point in my life. I am willing to look in the mirror and say: "Ah, this is where I need to change. This is unreality, and thus it is not part of me. I AM rising above it. I AM letting it go into the flame that I AM"

> Lanto dear, your Presence here,
> filling up my inner sphere.
> Life is now a sacred flow,
> God Wisdom I on all bestow.

> **O Holy Spirit, flow through me,**
> **I am the open door for thee.**
> **O mighty rushing stream of Light,**
> **transcendence is my sacred right.**

Sealing:

In the name of the Divine Mother, I fully accept that the power of these calls is used to set free the Ma-ter light, so it can outpicture the perfect vision of Christ for my own life, for all people and for the planet. In the name I AM THAT I AM, it is done! Amen.

6 | LET LOVE FLOW!

A dictation by Elohim Heros and Amora, representing the Third Ray of God's love.

We come in Oneness, known as Heros and Amora, Elohim of the Third Ray, to give you some understanding and – if you are willing – some direct experience of how love relates to communication from the heart.

Why did we have you give the *Invocation for Overcoming the Past* [See *www.transcendencetoolbox.com*] before this dictation on love? Consider how you were asked during this rosary to affirm radical forgiveness, unconditional forgiveness, of everything from the past—from yourself to other people, to God, to the Ma-ter light. When you are anchored in unconditional love, your past does not disappear but it ceases to have power over your present—and thus it also has no power over your future. Why is this, my beloved? Because when you are One with that flame, with that River of Life of unconditional love, you know that you are *more*, infinitely more than any manifestation from your past in this limited sphere here on earth.

You might have walked outside and seen a sunbeam reflected from a puddle on the road. That sunbeam does not identify itself with the puddle. It knows it is a sunbeam. Even though a sunbeam can be seen through a dirty window and be somewhat colored by that window, it is in your eyes that the sunbeam is colored whereas the sunbeam knows it is an extension of the Sun. You too are, of course, an extension of the Sun of your I AM Presence, even the Sun of your Creator. When you allow yourself to reconnect to that reality, you will feel the unconditional love of your Creator flowing through you. Then how can you identify yourself with any of the situations and conditions and events that have taken place in your past on this earth? You will know you are infinitely *more*. You will even know that other people are more than the manifestations of the past that you have experienced. You will be able to over-come the most common tendency that causes conflicts on earth, namely the tendency to hold on to a past image of oneself and of others, even a past image of the world and of God.

Your past becomes your database

Building on the discourse about wisdom and about the intellect – and how the intellect is designed to work with the world of form to detect differences, to categorize differences, to analyze causes in the world of form – you see that what happens to many people, in fact what happens to all people, is that they cre-ate a database in their subconscious minds. Most people are not even aware of this, but some are beginning to peel back that veil to be aware of how they have created these images in the past.

When that database is created, any new event is then instantly compared to the database. You meet another person, and instantly and subconsciously your mind seeks to label that person in order to know in which category, in which drawer from your past, you can place that person. You will then know how you are supposed to respond to that person based on how you have responded to other people from that category in the past.

In many cases you have people who meet each other for the first time – at least in this lifetime – and one would think that when you meet another person that you have never met before, you would meet that person on a blank slate, you would give that person an opportunity to be himself or herself. But most people cannot do this. They are instantly and subconsciously seeking to put that person in a neat, little category in the subconscious database. As soon as they have enough input from the person that their subconscious minds feel they can now label that person, well then, they are no longer responding to that person as a unique individual. They are responding the way they would have responded – and, indeed, the way they did respond – to similar people in the past.

The basis for conflict

This, of course, is how you see, in its extreme form, the conflict between various groups of people, such as based on skin color, race, or even the conflict between men and women. You meet a person and instantly you evaluate: "Is it a man or a woman?" Well then, I need to behave such and such. "Is that person black or white?" Well, then I need to behave such and such. "Is that person a Jew or any other race that I am familiar with?" Well then, my behavior must be adjusted accordingly.

Surely, if that person belongs to one of the millions of black people or the billions of women on this planet, well then that person must behave the way all the other people in that category do—or so the intellect reasons. It cannot connect, as was said yesterday, to the infinity, to the unconditionality of the River of Life, but can only relate to the limited world of form where everything is categorized by something. What is that something?

Study the intellectuals with wisdom

Here is where you need to use wisdom to study the intellectual people on this planet – those who think they know best – whether they are found in the field of science, in the field of government, or in the field of religion. Study them a little bit, and then go a little bit deeper. You will find that there are intellectual people – very intelligent people and often well-meaning – who are absolutely convinced, based on their intellectual reasoning, that science is the only true way to know reality, that there is nothing beyond the material universe and that all religion is simply an unreality conjured up by the mind.

Likewise, you will find people who are absolutely convinced, based on intellectual reasoning, that their political ideology or their political system is the only true one and it will bring God's kingdom or some other edenic state to earth. Of course, in the field of religion you find theologians who are absolutely convinced that their religion is the only true one, that all others are false, that science is false, that science has no validity, and so forth and so on.

What you realize when you look at this is that every person has a certain coloring, a certain world view, that sets the tone for that person's personal database. People are often very convinced that their database is not subjective, that their database is the only real way to look at life. Therefore, they never question that basic paradigm, that basic world view that is the very foundation for their database and thus colors everything in it.

Going into anti-love

What happens when people accept such a limited view is that they inevitably go into a vibration of anti-love. When you accept one particular limited view and elevate it to the status of infallibility – the only right one – well, then of course you cannot escape the fact that there are other views on earth. Therefore, you go into the dualistic struggle of having to defend your view against the opposing views or the competing views, sometimes even thinking you have to destroy those competing views, even destroy or kill the people who embody them or who have chosen to believe them.

This sense of being threatened by other viewpoints – by other limited beliefs, by other world views – is a sign of anti-love. It is a sign that you have been ensnared by the false teachers of anti-love, that you have absorbed the consciousness of anti-love, and that you have allowed that consciousness to influence – perhaps completely make up the very foundation for – your personal database. It has colored the very core of your world view, how you see the world, how you see God, how you see other people. It colors how you see yourself and how you relate to the world, other people and God, even how you relate to yourself, how you view yourself.

What I endeavor to explain here is that when you are in this state of mind, you cannot communicate from the heart. As we have said before, the heart is based on oneness—the core of your being is one with all life. In order to connect to that oneness – to accept that oneness, in order to let it flow through you and find expression through you – you must be willing to question your database, to question your world view, and to consider: "Is it based on love or is it based on anti-love?" You see, my beloved, true love, real love, living love, is unconditional.

Why love is misunderstood

If you look at the world, you will see that there is probably no other faculty or characteristic that is more misunderstood than love. The problem here is that people are trying to *understand* love. How do most people see understanding? They see it as an intellectual activity where you compare love to what you have in your database. Love will be colored by the world view that the person has as a foundation for the database, but it will also be colored by previous experiences of love – so to speak – on this planet.

The reality, however, is that very few people on this planet have experienced unconditional love in the physical realm. One might say that unconditional love in its purest form cannot be expressed currently on planet earth because of the density of the energies found here. Nevertheless, one can still see the expression of certain – almost reflections – of unconditional love. Most people have never experienced that, for they have only experienced conditional love that is precisely based on a person's database of how that person believes that love should be expressed or not expressed, based on their world view and their previous experiences.

Naturally, when people seek to understand love, they subconsciously seek to base that understanding on their database. But do you see what we have explained here? The database is designed or is created by the intellect, which is designed to deal with the world of form where everything is characterized by certain characteristics and limitations.

Love is unconditional. How can love ever be fit into a database designed to deal with the material world? Do you see? It is not possible to understand unconditional love in that way. Either people do not understand love – and many people give up – or they think they understand it. But they only understand their own creation of their own database that they project onto God.

Letting love flow

If you take a person on earth who is choosing to look at the Sun through red glasses and is absolutely convinced that the Sun is red, then because you do not see through the glasses but see the Sun as it appears in the sky, you will see that the person is obviously being silly. Do you also see that so many people on earth look at the world, look at love, through a particular colored lens? They insist that this is how love is, this is how life is, this is how God is, this is how other people are. These people cannot tune in to unconditional love. They cannot receive it, and they cannot experience it.

They cannot give it because they cannot let unconditional love be unconditional and flow through them and express itself unconditionally. Which does not mean that it is always the same, but means that in any given situation it expresses itself in a way that raises up the people in that situation, depending on their level of consciousness.

Instead, people seek to express love according to the images of love that they have in their database. This, of course, means that they must seek to control love. That means they shut themselves off from the River of Life, from the flow of unconditional love—which will not be controlled, which cannot be controlled, for then it would no longer be unconditional.

If you truly desire to communicate from the heart, you must ponder the unconditionality of true love compared to your view of love. You must be willing to question your personal database and see how it colors your view of love and thus actually prevents you from opening your being to the flow of unconditional love, even the very experience that you are loved unconditionally.

What you do to others

As Christ said: "Do unto others what you want them to do to you." The underlying meaning being that what you do onto others shows what you have already done to yourself—subconsciously. When you create a database and use it to judge other people, is it not obvious that the first person to be put in the database is yourself?

You, naturally, must already have judged yourself before you start projecting that judgment outside yourself towards others. When you judge others, then you put yourself in a mental box that prevents you from experiencing that you are loved unconditionally by your Source. Therefore, of course, you cannot experience unconditional love but are bound to repeat the endless cycle of seeking to justify your version of conditional love.

What can break the stalemate? What can break the catch-22? Well, it certainly helps to use the understanding of the mind – not the intellectual, but the higher understanding – to recognize what we are talking about, to recognize the need to simply go beyond that database and to step back from the filters. You then step back until you are so far back that you can see beyond the filters, and you can begin to get a glimpse of the world that is beyond the filter, the real world.

Then you can see the Sun as it really is, you can see your higher being as it really is, and thus experience the unconditional love that your higher being has for you. You can then come to the absolute, stunning awakening where you recognize that your I AM Presence does not see the world through the filter you have created in your lower mind. This is not something that a person can do instantly, even if confronted with this teaching. It can take many years, even many lifetimes, for a person to gradually separate itself from the ego to the critical level where the person's conscious self begins to recognize that the ego is not always right.

Your ego has no influence over reality

Look at some of the people in the world who are totally caught up in a particular conflict. These are the people for whom their conscious selves completely identify with their egos and their egos' view of the world. For them it is a matter of life and death to defend their religion or their political ideology, even by killing other people in order to do so.

You have, of course, as spiritual people, begun that separation from the ego where you see that the ego is not always right. It is wise to consider that there are subtleties to this and that it is necessary for all spiritual people to actually come to that absolute, undeniable moment of truth where you recognize – you experience – the limitations of the ego.

Think back to when people during the Middle Ages believed the universe was very small and that the earth was the center of the universe. Then think how you today have grown up realizing that this earth is like an infinitely small speck of dust in a very, very large universe with billions of galaxies. Then look at the fact that there are billions of people on this planet who are still caught up in the belief that by praying to God or performing certain rituals, they can actually control God and get him to do something for them.

This is the recognition you need to come to—that your ego has absolutely no power over reality. No matter how convinced your ego is that its view of the world is reality, it is still a complete illusion. Outside of the ego's own little parallel universe, there is the real world that is in no way, shape or form affected by this—as the Sun is not affected by anything that takes place on earth. Do you think the Sun is affected at all by the fact that it is a cloudy day right now? Surely, you realize that there may be a few clouds over your own place here but that there are vast stretches of the earth where there are no clouds.

Unconditional love knows no conditionality

When you are caught in looking at the world from a certain perspective – where you are trapped in thinking that your little ego and your little database is the center of the universe – you cannot experience unconditional love. That unconditional love is unconditional—which means it is given to all people on earth 24 hours a day, my beloved.

You cannot actually place yourself in any sphere – be it in the material universe or another realm – where you are cut off from the unconditional love of God. It is not possible. How can you shut out something that is unconditional? It penetrates all conditions! You may think you are cut off from it, but you are only cut off from it because you are seeing the world through the database that says: "Love is such and such, and it is not this or that."

When you communicate with other people, you are, of course, communicating with another person through your personal database. The other person is communicating with you through his or her personal database. That is why you will see that people with vastly different databases often clash. That is why you will see that people tend to congregate together with people who have similar databases so they can avoid the worst of the conflicts. But you see, coming together with people who have similar illusions as yourself is not helping you rise above those limitations. On the contrary, by reinforcing the validity of each others illusions, many of the spiritual and religious people around the world are actually helping each other hold back their progress—they convince each other that their view of reality is the only true one.

Do not set yourselves apart

We have purposely not given this movement a very strongly defined profile. We do not want you to build that sense that you are different from all other spiritual people, thereby thinking you are, of course, better because you have this or that higher teaching. We desire you to be the ones who are willing to communicate from the heart by first tuning in to your higher being and allowing the manifestation of that experience of unconditional love so that you know through experience – not through intellectual reasoning, but through direct experience – that you are *more* than this material manifestation.

Then you have the option, when you meet another, to build a habit of not responding to that other person's outer words, outer actions, even the person's outer vibration, the person's state of consciousness. Instead, you can build a habit of tuning in to your own infinite self. You can even recognize that the other person – no matter what their outer appearance or manifestation may be – also has an infinite self.

If you sense any kind of conflict with a person, you can ask your infinite self to communicate with that person's infinite self and as much as possible bring that understanding of oneness to the other person's conscious awareness. You will see how misunderstandings or conflicts can be resolved overnight by the person coming to a new awareness. Of course, also by you coming to the new awareness that you are not enemies. You are surely connected in the infinite world, even though you may appear to be very disconnected in this material, illusory realm.

How the database traps you

The effect of people's databases is that at any given moment the subconscious mind is hard at work comparing everything that happens to something in the database. What is in the database is what has happened in the past. Therefore, you are not experiencing the present moment as it is. You are not experiencing reality. You are not experiencing it with the innocent mind of a child, as Jesus said.

You are experiencing it through the filter of your past. You are not actually experiencing the present. You are projecting an image upon it based on your database. Everything in the material realm is made from the Ma-ter light, which is designed to serve as the cosmic mirror that reflects back to you what you project into it. If you allow your past to project onto the present moment that this world is a place with many unkind people who are out to get you, well then you will attract people to you who are willing to play that role.

They might have a need based on the fact that they think the world is a place with many people who are victims, or who do not want to make decisions for themselves so they need other people to shake them up and tell them what to do. Like attracts like in the sense that a person who has the need to control will attract someone who has a need to be controlled, to be the victim.

When will you be free? You will be free when you become willing to look at your database and look at what is contained in all of those file folders in your subconscious file cabinet. You then go in and do some housecleaning and pull out the old pieces of paper and see that the receipt from the drugstore from 15 years ago really doesn't need to be there anymore. Likewise, that decision you made based on what happened 15 lifetimes ago doesn't need to be there either.

Be willing to experience unconditional love

The essence of what we seek to communicate here is that you can only communicate from the heart when you have some experience of unconditional love and when you are willing to extend that unconditional love to others. You are willing to not judge them, to not label them, but to allow them to be who they are at the present moment. You also allow yourself, as Master MORE explained, to be who you are regardless of who they choose to be, realizing that you can choose your reaction independently of their state of mind.

If you do not do this, then you are allowing all of the other people in the past who treated you a certain way to determine – to decide – your reaction to that person who seems to be treating you in a similar way. But that person is just expressing his or her state of consciousness independently of all the others. There is no connection between that person who is here now and all the persons that you encountered in the past, there is no objective connection out there. There is only the connection in your consciousness that you keep attracting a certain kind of people to you because you have not resolved the filter in your database that says the world is populated by those kind of people.

Communication from the heart is an expression of unconditional love. Unconditional love means that you are free from the past. This does not mean that you have no memory of what has happened in the past. It means that you do not have the emotional scars and wounds or the mental beliefs that cause you to go into a certain reactionary pattern when you encounter a person that pushes the buttons from the past.

Meet the present in the now

You have no buttons. You can say: "Regardless of what has happened in my past, in this present moment I AM not reliving my past. I AM meeting this present moment on a clean slate with the innocent mind of the child." By doing this, you set yourself free to not repeat these old reactionary patterns, but to find a higher response to a situation you have encountered before. When you demonstrate your willingness to find a higher response, you will be open to the flow of unconditional love because now you will not seek to protect yourself, to limit others. You will instead seek to raise up others, and that is the condition for being open to the flow of unconditional love.

Did you catch the seeming contradiction in my words? There is a condition to being open to the flow of unconditional love. But the condition is that you have no conditions—that you will let love flow and express itself unconditionally. It is when you are trapped in the conditions based on the database and the past that you want to control how love expresses itself through you. It is then that you shut off the flow by setting up conditions for love's expression. Unconditional love must step back and say: "I respect your choice. But I will be here at any moment you decide to change that choice and allow me to flow through you."

You gain only by giving

Can you now pull this together in your minds and see two very important conclusions? Unconditional love wants to flow for the raising of all life. If you have set up conditions in your mind and used them to judge other people, then you will say: "I cannot express love to any person unless that person lives up to a certain standard. If people do not live up to that standard, they need to be punished or controlled." You are not giving love freely and unconditionally, and when you are not giving love to others freely, then love cannot flow through you—and thus you cannot experience unconditional love.

Do you see, as is said again in a hidden sentence in this rosary: "For what I give, I surely gain?" If you want forgiveness, give forgiveness to others. If you want love, give love to others—but give it unconditionally. Forgive people unconditionally and you will be forgiven unconditionally. Did not Christ say: Judge not, lest you be judged, for what you mete out to others shall be meted out to yourself, for the universe is but a mirror.

Be willing to see that if you are not experiencing unconditional love, it is because there is some condition in your subconscious database that is restricting its flow. You are seeking to control it because you are seeking to restrict other people in order to make them conform to your world view so that you do not feel that your world view is threatened. Be willing to not only question the world view, but be willing to consider that you can come to a point where you give it up. Look again at the people who are identified with their belief system. Many of them cannot suddenly give up their belief system because if they did, they would be thrown into an identity crisis, not knowing who they are.

The reality of spirituality

The reality of the spiritual path is that you gradually move towards the point where you can do what Jesus did on the cross. He suddenly saw in a flash that even though he had attained a high degree of Christhood in that embodiment, he had retained certain expectations of how things should unfold. Those expectations kept him tied to the earth. Then, he decided – in that final act of surrender – to give up the ghosts of the past, and that was why he was resurrected.

Had he not given up the ghosts on the cross, what do you think would have happened? He would have had to re-embody to again outlive those ghosts until he was willing to question the way he looked at the world and realize that it was unreality.

There are those who think that Jesus was God or the Son of God from the beginning and that his victory and ascension were guaranteed. Nothing can be guaranteed in the world of free will. Jesus could have refused – on the cross – to give up those ghosts and therefore not become Jesus the Christ. Once again, we refer to what some people called Jesus the carpenter, although truth be told, Jesus was never a carpenter in that embodiment.

Give people a real choice

The goal of the spiritual path can be described as overcoming your conditions until you simply see the world as it *is*, accept it as it is, accept that what *is*, is an expression of unreality, that unreality can never be permanent. Therefore, in any situation, you allow that unconditional love to be expressed so as to give other people an opportunity to choose love over anti-love.

You do not go into the vibration of anti-love or seek to force them to make a certain choice. You give them the opportunity to make the choice. You are willing to let love be very direct – if necessary – in confronting them with that choice, in demonstrating very clearly – if necessary – that they have a different option. But you do not cross that boundary of seeking to force them. You remain free so that you can be in unconditional love no matter what they choose.

Of course, you may have the best of intentions of helping another – and you may put great effort into helping another person see something – and then they choose not to see it, and how do you feel? Well, if you feel any negativity, any attachment, you are not fully in unconditional love and then you have work to do on yourself. You need to look at the database and see why you have created an image that the beings around you – whom you know God has given complete free will – should respond a certain way, should make certain choices based on your actions or words. Why have you allowed yourself to incorporate those elements of anti-love in your database, in your world view?

Certainly, if you did not have such expectations, you could not be disappointed by other people no matter what they do or do not do. Do you see that only when you cannot be disappointed or otherwise affected negatively by other people, only then are you truly free. Only then are you in unconditional love. How can you be free, my beloved? Only by being in unconditional love. Only when there are no conditions, can you be truly free.

Receive my Presence

Beyond the words spoken, I have anchored our Presence as the masculine and feminine elements, the masculine and feminine expressions, of the Third Ray of God Love. You have had an opportunity to experience it, if you have been willing. If you have not experienced it, then consider that my Presence is beyond any limitations in the material universe. At any moment in the future, you can experience my Presence when you are willing to open your heart to it. If you cannot open your heart now, do not be discouraged, do not allow your subconscious database to create some kind of judgment. Recognize that you have some work to do to clean out some of the conditions that prevent you from accepting unconditional love, accepting that you are worthy to receive it. Then work on it, and recognize that whenever you reach the critical mass of cleaning out the file drawers, the Sun of unconditional love will shine through the clouds and you will experience it.

I AM beyond time and space, my beloved. You, too, are beyond time and space. You are currently choosing to identify yourself based on the limitations of time and space, which is perfectly acceptable—but it is not your only option.

In the Flame of Unconditional Love that I AM, I seal you. I seal the movements of spiritual people seeking a higher state of consciousness. As long as you remain dedicated to unconditional love, then the prince of this world will come and have nothing in you. Although his representatives may gain entry, they will not be able to take this movement down. They will not be able to stop the ascending spiral that has been created and has the potential to accelerate and become a glowing light in the darkness that still engulfs this planet. This is a light that will show the way to a new reality, a new way to associate with each other, a new way to communicate based on unconditional love. *Be sealed in that love.*

7 | I INVOKE
UNCONDITIONAL LOVE

In the name I AM THAT I AM, Jesus Christ, I call to my I AM Presence to flow through the I Will Be Presence that I AM and give this invocation with full power. I call to beloved Elohim Heros and Amora, Archangel Chamuel and Charity, and Paul the Venetian to help me overcome all blocks to my ability to communicate from love in all situations. Help me be free from all patterns or forces within or without that oppose my communication from the heart and my oneness with my I AM Presence, including ...

[Make personal calls]

I. I surrender all past images

1. I AM anchored in unconditional love. My past has no power over my present, and it has no power over my future.

> O Heros-Amora, in your love so pink,
> I care not what others about me may think,
> in oneness with you, I claim a new day,
> an innocent child, I frolic and play.

> **O Heros-Amora, a new life begun,**
> **I laugh at the devil, the serious one,**
> **I bathe in your glorious Ruby-Pink Sun,**
> **knowing my God allows life to be fun.**

2. I AM One with the flame, with the River of Life of unconditional love. I know I am *more*, infinitely more than any manifestation from my past in this limited sphere on earth.

> O Heros-Amora, life is such a joy,
> I see that the world is like a great toy,
> whatever my mind into it projects,
> the mirror of life exactly reflects.

> **O Heros-Amora, I reap what I sow,**
> **yet this is Plan B for helping me grow,**
> **for truly, Plan A is that I join the flow,**
> **immersed in the Infinite Love you bestow.**

3. I AM an extension of the Sun of my I AM Presence, even the Sun of my Creator. I allow myself to reconnect to that reality, and I feel the unconditional love of my Creator flowing through me.

O Heros-Amora, conditions you burn,
I know I AM free to take a new turn,
Immersed in the stream of infinite Love,
I know that my Spirit came from Above.

**O Heros-Amora, awakened I see,
in true love is no conditionality,
the devil is stuck in his duality,
but I AM set free by Love's reality.**

4. I no longer identify myself with any of the situations, conditions and events that have taken place in my past on this earth. I know I am infinitely *more*. I know other people are more than the manifestations of their past.

O Heros-Amora, I feel that at last,
I've risen above the trap of my past,
in true love I claim my freedom to grow,
forever I'm one with Love's Infinite Flow.

**O Heros-Amora, conditions are ties,
forming a net of serpentine lies,
your love has no bounds, forever it flies,
raising all life into Ruby-Pink skies.**

5. I unconditionally surrender any and all past images of myself and of others, even all past images of the world and of God.

> O Heros-Amora, in your love so pink,
> I care not what others about me may think,
> in oneness with you, I claim a new day,
> an innocent child, I frolic and play.

> **O Heros-Amora, a new life begun,**
> **I laugh at the devil, the serious one,**
> **I bathe in your glorious Ruby-Pink Sun,**
> **knowing my God allows life to be fun.**

6. I unconditionally surrender the coloring, the world view, that sets the tone for my personal database. I am willing to question the basic paradigm that is the foundation for my database and thus colors everything in it.

> O Heros-Amora, life is such a joy,
> I see that the world is like a great toy,
> whatever my mind into it projects,
> the mirror of life exactly reflects.

> **O Heros-Amora, I reap what I sow,**
> **yet this is Plan B for helping me grow,**
> **for truly, Plan A is that I join the flow,**
> **immersed in the Infinite Love you bestow.**

7. I unconditionally surrender all world views that cause me to go into a vibration of anti-love. I surrender the world view that I am a separate being and thus threatened by other people's world views.

O Heros-Amora, conditions you burn,
I know I AM free to take a new turn,
Immersed in the stream of infinite Love,
I know that my Spirit came from Above.

O Heros-Amora, awakened I see,
in true love is no conditionality,
the devil is stuck in his duality,
but I AM set free by Love's reality.

8. I unconditionally surrender all elements of the consciousness of anti-love that influence, even make up the foundation of, my personal database.

O Heros-Amora, I feel that at last,
I've risen above the trap of my past,
in true love I claim my freedom to grow,
forever I'm one with Love's Infinite Flow.

O Heros-Amora, conditions are ties,
forming a net of serpentine lies,
your love has no bounds, forever it flies,
raising all life into Ruby-Pink skies.

9. I am willing to communicate from the heart, to communicate from oneness and love. I am willing to question my database, to question my world view, and to consider: "Is it based on love or is it based on anti-love?"

Accelerate into Oneness, I AM real,
Accelerate into Oneness, all life heal,
Accelerate into Oneness, I AM MORE,
Accelerate into Oneness, all will soar.

Accelerate into Oneness! (3X)
Beloved Heros and Amora.
Accelerate into Oneness! (3X)
Beloved Chamuel and Charity.
Accelerate into Oneness! (3X)
Beloved Paul the Venetian.
Accelerate into Oneness! (3X)
Beloved I AM.

2. I am open to unconditional love

1. I am willing to experience unconditional love in the physical realm. I surrender all tendency to want love to fit into the conditions in my database. I surrender those conditions.

> Chamuel Archangel, in ruby ray power,
> I know I am taking a life-giving shower.
> Love burning away all perversions of will,
> I suddenly feel my desires falling still.

Chamuel Archangel, descend from Above,
Chamuel Archangel, with ruby-pink love,
Chamuel Archangel, so often thought-of,
Chamuel Archangel, o come Holy Dove.

2. I acknowledge that love is unconditional. I surrender all desire to understand unconditional love, all tendency to project the images from the material realm unto love. I want to experience the real thing, not an image from my own subconscious database.

> Chamuel Archangel, a spiral of light,
> as ruby ray fire now pierces the night.
> All forces of darkness consumed by your fire,
> consuming all those who will not rise higher.

Chamuel Archangel, descend from Above,
Chamuel Archangel, with ruby-pink love,
Chamuel Archangel, so often thought-of,
Chamuel Archangel, o come Holy Dove.

3. I am tuning in to unconditional love and I am willing to receive it. I am letting unconditional love be unconditional and flow through me and express itself unconditionally. I am letting love express itself in a way that raises up people, depending on their level of consciousness.

> Chamuel Archangel, your love so immense,
> with clarified vision, my life now makes sense.
> The purpose of life you so clearly reveal,
> immersed in your love, God's oneness I feel.

> **Chamuel Archangel, descend from Above,**
> **Chamuel Archangel, with ruby-pink love,**
> **Chamuel Archangel, so often thought-of,**
> **Chamuel Archangel, o come Holy Dove.**

4. I unconditionally surrender the ego's desire to control love. I immerse myself in the River of Life, in the flow of unconditional love—which will not be controlled, which cannot be controlled, for then it would no longer be unconditional.

> Chamuel Archangel, what calmness you bring,
> I see now that even death has no sting.
> For truly, in love there can be no decay,
> as love is transcendence into a new day.

> **Chamuel Archangel, descend from Above,**
> **Chamuel Archangel, with ruby-pink love,**
> **Chamuel Archangel, so often thought-of,**
> **Chamuel Archangel, o come Holy Dove.**

5. I desire to communicate from the heart, and I am willing to experience the unconditionality of true love compared to the ego's view of love. I am opening my being to the flow of unconditional love, even the very experience that I am loved unconditionally.

> Chamuel Archangel, in ruby ray power,
> I know I am taking a life-giving shower.
> Love burning away all perversions of will,
> I suddenly feel my desires falling still.

> **Chamuel Archangel, descend from Above,**
> **Chamuel Archangel, with ruby-pink love,**
> **Chamuel Archangel, so often thought-of,**
> **Chamuel Archangel, o come Holy Dove.**

6. I acknowledge that when I create a database and use it to judge other people, I am the first person to be put into the database. I unconditionally surrender all tendency to judge myself and others. I surrender the endless cycle of seeking to justify my version of conditional love.

> Chamuel Archangel, a spiral of light,
> as ruby ray fire now pierces the night.
> All forces of darkness consumed by your fire,
> consuming all those who will not rise higher.

> **Chamuel Archangel, descend from Above,**
> **Chamuel Archangel, with ruby-pink love,**
> **Chamuel Archangel, so often thought-of,**
> **Chamuel Archangel, o come Holy Dove.**

7. I am willing to experience my I AM Presence as it really is. I experience the unconditional love that my Presence has for me. I am awakened to the fact that my I AM Presence does not see the world through the limitations of my ego.

Chamuel Archangel, your love so immense,
with clarified vision, my life now makes sense.
The purpose of life you so clearly reveal,
immersed in your love, God's oneness I feel.

Chamuel Archangel, descend from Above,
Chamuel Archangel, with ruby-pink love,
Chamuel Archangel, so often thought-of,
Chamuel Archangel, o come Holy Dove.

8. Beloved I AM Presence, awaken me to the recognition that my ego has absolutely no power over reality. No matter how convinced my ego is that its view of the world is reality, it is still a complete illusion. I want to experience the real world outside the ego's parallel universe.

Chamuel Archangel, what calmness you bring,
I see now that even death has no sting.
For truly, in love there can be no decay,
as love is transcendence into a new day.

Chamuel Archangel, descend from Above,
Chamuel Archangel, with ruby-pink love,
Chamuel Archangel, so often thought-of,
Chamuel Archangel, o come Holy Dove.

9. I acknowledge that unconditional love is unconditional. It is given to all people on earth 24 hours a day. I recognize that I am never cut off from the unconditional love of God. The ego cannot shut out something that is unconditional, for it penetrates all conditions! I accept God's unconditional love for me.

> With angels I soar,
> as I reach for MORE.
> The angels so real,
> their love all will heal.
> The angels bring peace,
> all conflicts will cease.
> With angels of light,
> we soar to new height.

> **The rustling sound of angel wings,**
> **what joy as even matter sings,**
> **what joy as every atom rings,**
> **in harmony with angel wings.**

3. I rise above conflict

1. When I meet another, I will not respond to that person based on outer appearances, even the person's state of consciousness. Instead, I will tune in to my infinite self. I recognize that the other person also has an infinite self.

> O Heros-Amora, in your love so pink,
> I care not what others about me may think,
> in oneness with you, I claim a new day,
> an innocent child, I frolic and play.

> **O Heros-Amora, a new life begun,**
> **I laugh at the devil, the serious one,**
> **I bathe in your glorious Ruby-Pink Sun,**
> **knowing my God allows life to be fun.**

2. Whenever I sense conflict, I ask my infinite self to communicate with that person's infinite self and as much as possible bring that understanding of oneness to my own and the other person's conscious awareness.

> O Heros-Amora, life is such a joy,
> I see that the world is like a great toy,
> whatever my mind into it projects,
> the mirror of life exactly reflects.

> **O Heros-Amora, I reap what I sow,**
> **yet this is Plan B for helping me grow,**
> **for truly, Plan A is that I join the flow,**
> **immersed in the Infinite Love you bestow.**

3. I recognize that what is in my personal database is what has happened in the past. I am willing to experience the present moment as it is. I am willing to experience reality. I am willing to experience everything with the innocent mind of a child.

O Heros-Amora, conditions you burn,
I know I AM free to take a new turn,
Immersed in the stream of infinite Love,
I know that my Spirit came from Above.

O Heros-Amora, awakened I see,
in true love is no conditionality,
the devil is stuck in his duality,
but I AM set free by Love's reality.

4. I want to be free from my past. I am willing to look at my database and look at what is contained in all of those file folders in my subconscious file cabinet. I AM Presence, help me do some housecleaning and let go of all conditional images.

O Heros-Amora, I feel that at last,
I've risen above the trap of my past,
in true love I claim my freedom to grow,
forever I'm one with Love's Infinite Flow.

O Heros-Amora, conditions are ties,
forming a net of serpentine lies,
your love has no bounds, forever it flies,
raising all life into Ruby-Pink skies.

5. I am willing to communicate from the heart, I am willing to experience unconditional love and extend that unconditional love to others. I am willing to not judge them, to not label them, but to allow them to be who they are at the present moment.

> O Heros-Amora, in your love so pink,
> I care not what others about me may think,
> in oneness with you, I claim a new day,
> an innocent child, I frolic and play.

> **O Heros-Amora, a new life begun,**
> **I laugh at the devil, the serious one,**
> **I bathe in your glorious Ruby-Pink Sun,**
> **knowing my God allows life to be fun.**

6. I am willing to allow myself to be who I am, regardless of who other people choose to be or what I have chosen in the past. I fully acknowledge the power of choice. I can choose my reaction independently of my past or of other people's state of mind.

> O Heros-Amora, life is such a joy,
> I see that the world is like a great toy,
> whatever my mind into it projects,
> the mirror of life exactly reflects.

> **O Heros-Amora, I reap what I sow,**
> **yet this is Plan B for helping me grow,**
> **for truly, Plan A is that I join the flow,**
> **immersed in the Infinite Love you bestow.**

7. I unconditionally surrender all tendency to allow my past to determine my reaction in the present. I surrender the filter in my database that causes me to attract a certain type of people.

O Heros-Amora, conditions you burn,
I know I AM free to take a new turn,
Immersed in the stream of infinite Love,
I know that my Spirit came from Above.

O Heros-Amora, awakened I see,
in true love is no conditionality,
the devil is stuck in his duality,
but I AM set free by Love's reality.

8. I recognize that communication from the heart is an expression of unconditional love. Unconditional love means that I am free from the past. I am willing to be healed of all emotional scars, wounds and mental beliefs that cause me to go into a certain reactionary pattern when someone pushes the buttons from the past.

O Heros-Amora, I feel that at last,
I've risen above the trap of my past,
in true love I claim my freedom to grow,
forever I'm one with Love's Infinite Flow.

O Heros-Amora, conditions are ties,
forming a net of serpentine lies,
your love has no bounds, forever it flies,
raising all life into Ruby-Pink skies.

9. Centered in my I AM Presence, I say: "Regardless of what has happened in my past, in this present moment I AM not reliving my past. I AM meeting this present moment on a clean slate with the innocent mind of the child." I am willing to see a higher response to any situation.

Accelerate into Oneness, I AM real,
Accelerate into Oneness, all life heal,
Accelerate into Oneness, I AM MORE,
Accelerate into Oneness, all will soar.

Accelerate into Oneness! (3X)
Beloved Heros and Amora.
Accelerate into Oneness! (3X)
Beloved Chamuel and Charity.
Accelerate into Oneness! (3X)
Beloved Paul the Venetian.
Accelerate into Oneness! (3X)
Beloved I AM.

4. I am letting love flow

1. I am willing to find a higher response based on unconditional love. I will not seek to protect myself or limit others. I seek to raise up others, and thus I am open to the flow of unconditional love.

> Master Paul, venetian dream,
> your love for beauty's flowing stream.
> Master Paul, in love's own womb,
> your power shatters ego's tomb.

> **O Holy Spirit, flow through me,**
> **I am the open door for thee.**
> **O mighty rushing stream of Light,**
> **transcendence is my sacred right.**

2. I unconditionally surrender the ego's tendency to say that I cannot express love to any person unless that person lives up to a certain standard. I am giving love freely and unconditionally. I am allowing love to flow through me, for I am willing to experience unconditional love.

> Master Paul, your counsel wise,
> my mind is raised to lofty skies.
> Master Paul, in wisdom's love,
> such beauty flowing from Above.

> **O Holy Spirit, flow through me,**
> **I am the open door for thee.**
> **O mighty rushing stream of Light,**
> **transcendence is my sacred right.**

3. I acknowledge that what I give, I surely gain. I give forgiveness to others, I give love to others—and I give it unconditionally. I forgive people unconditionally and I accept that God forgives me unconditionally.

Master Paul, love is an art,
it opens up the secret heart.
Master Paul, love's rushing flow,
my heart awash in sacred glow.

**O Holy Spirit, flow through me,
I am the open door for thee.
O mighty rushing stream of Light,
transcendence is my sacred right.**

4. I acknowledge that if I am not experiencing unconditional love, it is because there is some condition in my subconscious database that is restricting its flow. I unconditionally surrender my ego-based, conditional world view.

Master Paul, accelerate,
upon pure love I meditate.
Master Paul, intentions pure,
my self-transcendence will ensure.

**O Holy Spirit, flow through me,
I am the open door for thee.
O mighty rushing stream of Light,
transcendence is my sacred right.**

5. I am willing to do what Jesus did on the cross. I am willing to see the expectations that keep me tied to the earth. I am willing to unconditionally surrender the ghosts of the past and be resurrected into a higher sense of self.

Master Paul, your love will heal,
my inner light you do reveal.
Master Paul, all life console,
with you I'm being truly whole.

**O Holy Spirit, flow through me,
I am the open door for thee.
O mighty rushing stream of Light,
transcendence is my sacred right.**

6. I unconditionally surrender all conditions, for I am willing to see the world as it is, accept it as it is, accept that what is is an expression of unreality and that unreality can never be permanent. In any situation, I allow unconditional love to be expressed so as to give other people an opportunity to choose love over anti-love.

Master Paul, you serve the All,
by helping us transcend the fall.
Master Paul, in peace we rise,
as ego meets its sure demise.

**O Holy Spirit, flow through me,
I am the open door for thee.
O mighty rushing stream of Light,
transcendence is my sacred right.**

7. I will not go into the vibration of anti-love and seek to force others to make a certain choice. I give them the opportunity to make the choice and then set them and myself free. I am willing to let love be very direct, yet I remain free so that I can be in unconditional love no matter what others choose.

Master Paul, love all life free,
your love is for eternity.
Master Paul, you are the One,
to help us make the journey fun.

O Holy Spirit, flow through me,
I am the open door for thee.
O mighty rushing stream of Light,
transcendence is my sacred right.

8. I accept and absorb the Presence of the masculine and feminine elements, the masculine and feminine expressions, of the Third Ray of God Love. I am willing to experience the fullness of unconditional love. I accept that love is beyond time and space, and I am beyond time and space.

Master Paul, you balance all,
the seven rays upon my call.
Master Paul, you paint the sky,
with colors that delight the I.

O Holy Spirit, flow through me,
I am the open door for thee.
O mighty rushing stream of Light,
transcendence is my sacred right.

9. I fully accept that I am in the ascending spiral of unconditional love. I am willing to accelerate and become a glowing light in the darkness on this planet. My I AM Presence is the light that will show the way to a new reality, a new way to communicate based on unconditional love. I accept that I AM sealed in that love.

> Master Paul, your Presence here,
> filling up my inner sphere.
> Life is now a sacred flow,
> God Love I do on all bestow.

> **O Holy Spirit, flow through me,**
> **I am the open door for thee.**
> **O mighty rushing stream of Light,**
> **transcendence is my sacred right.**

Sealing:

In the name of the Divine Mother, I fully accept that the power of these calls is used to set free the Ma-ter light, so it can outpicture the perfect vision of Christ for my own life, for all people and for the planet. In the name I AM THAT I AM, it is done! Amen.

8 | YOUR REAL SELF IS STILL PURE

A dictation by Elohim Purity and Astrea, representing the Fourth Ray of God's Purity.

Purity and Astrea, Astrea and Purity, Elohim of the Fourth Ray. We are here because you have earned the Presence of the Elohim of Purity by being willing to purify yourselves, my beloved. You have been willing to take a look at the imperfect images in the database, throw out those that limited you, and move beyond them. It is only impurities that can prevent you from being who you truly are in God. One of the most effective weapons used by those who seek to control people on earth is precisely to expose them to various kinds of impurities and perversions—and then somehow get people to feel that they are obligated to take this in and obligated to somehow hold on to it.

How can holding on to earth get you to heaven?

As an example, take the belief so prevalent in the Middle East that when someone has wronged you, you need to respond in kind. You need to seek revenge, you need to hold a negative, judgmental view of that other person, or those other people, that other race, that other nation, that other religion. You are obligated to hold on to that negativity, for somehow, sometime, it will qualify you to enter the kingdom of God. Do you not see that all spiritual teachers, including Mohamed, Moses, Abraham, Jesus, the Buddha, Lao Tzu, and all other spiritual teachers have always stated that in order to enter the kingdom of God, you must let go of the human, the human impurities.

How can people continue to believe that by holding on to impurities – and holding on to an imperfect image of other people – they will qualify to enter the Kingdom of Purity? Of course, they do not actually believe this, as I have stated it here. They have never thought about it the way I AM stating it here, being misled by the false teachers, by the blind leaders, into never thinking deeply about their beliefs and whether those beliefs are consistent, whether they make sense, whether they actually compare to the scriptures of the religion that they profess to follow. So many people on earth have become so overwhelmed, have allowed their subconscious database to be so filled to overflowing with these impurities, that they cannot think clearly about themselves, about life, about their belief and their religion.

Two forms of impurity

Impurity, takes two primary forms. There is the perversion of the father in the form of impure images, ideas and beliefs. There is the perversion of the mother in the form of impure feelings, impure energies. Of course, when people come to accept an impure belief or image, then they become susceptible to generating impure feelings. At the same time they feel that because of the imperfect belief, their impure feelings are justified in this instance. "These other people really are against God, and therefore it is justified that I hate them and seek revenge over them."

There is no other way, they think. They are so overwhelmed by this combination of imperfect beliefs and imperfect feelings that are interwoven and therefore reinforce each other, keeping the soul mesmerized, transfixed so that it cannot simply step back and say: "Why are we doing this? Why are we continuing to do this 5,000 years after we started? Why? Why is there still war in the Middle East? Why has there been war in the Middle East for all of known history? How can it ever change as long as we hold on to these impure feelings, these impure beliefs?"

The Middle East is the region of the world that has the greatest concentration of impurity, impure beliefs, impure feelings, hatred, anger, revenge. There is the belief that one group of people are superior to another, that their religion is superior to all others, that they somehow are the chosen people. No matter how they behave, God will let them into his kingdom and even send to hell those who are not of their race or religion, but who actually behave according to the prescripts of their religion. These people are failing to see that they themselves are not behaving according to their religion, for they are indeed allowing these impure feelings that their own religion clearly condemns— or states will not be acceptable in the eyes of God.

The progression of the seven rays

Relating this understanding of impurities to communication from the heart, do you see that there is a certain progression in the seven rays? Take a person who has descended into the duality consciousness and has been entrapped in various kinds of impurities. For that person to turn around and start the upward path, the person must come to a point of having the will to change. This may come as a result of experiencing such negative circumstances that the person finally realizes that this simply cannot continue—and then realizes: "I must change. I cannot keep doing this." It may be as the result of understanding, of vision, of inspiration, of seeing the example of someone who has changed their life. It may be any number of things, but there has to be a willingness to change.

Then comes, of course, the need for an understanding of how to change and what needs to change. Then comes the need for love, for unless you realize that there is more to you than the impure self, how can you even begin to let go of the impure self? If your sense of identity, if your container of self, is filled with impurities so that you cannot see that there is more to you than the mortal self, you will think that if you let go of the impurities, then you will lose part of your identity, you will lose your mortal self.

Indeed, my beloved, some of you might have noticed that when you start making calls about letting the mortal self die – about releasing the separate self – you feel a certain fear, anger, animosity, resentment towards doing this. Certainly not your own, but that of the world, especially the Middle East where actually many people believe that if they were to follow the prompting of Christ to turn the other cheek, they would lose the identity they have built as being powerful people.

Misunderstanding power

There is hardly a region on the earth where there is a greater mis-understanding of power than the Middle East. There are people in the Middle East who worship God because they see God as powerful, as all powerful. If they were to contemplate the fem-inine aspect of God or contemplate the love or the wisdom of God, they would feel that that could not be the real God. The real God, according to their view, must be powerful, almost like the tyrants they have attracted to themselves over the centuries. They actually believe that these tyrants, who rule on the earth, are doing so because they have the same power that God would use to rule them, as he demands blind obedience to some rule or some law written down in a book—rather than calling them to go into their hearts and have obedience to the flow of the River of Life.

Unless you have attuned to the love – unless you have experienced the love of that greater part of yourself – you cannot let go of the outer identity. How can you then take the next step and come up to the Fourth Ray of purity where you can – based on the will, the wisdom, and the love attained on the first three rays – start objectively, calmly looking at yourself and evaluating: "What is pure? What is impure in my consciousness?" Then recognizing that if you are to progress further on the path, you must let go of the impurities, you must let go of that which is impure. That which is impure cannot enter the kingdom of God. As long as it remains in your forcefield, in your mind, well then *you* cannot enter the kingdom of God, my beloved.

The screen door to heaven

You might consider the image that many of you have of a screen in front of your window, set up so that insects cannot enter your house. The screen is not solid, it has openings, small openings. The wind, indeed the winds of the Holy Spirit, can pass through the openings and can enter. Anything carried with the wind, be it insects or leaves or anything else, cannot enter. They hit the screen and fall down. Likewise, there is a screen in front of the doorway to the kingdom of heaven. As long as you have impurities in your forcefield – in your mind, in your being – those impurities will hit the screen. If you are so identified with them that you cannot let them go, how can you enter the kingdom of

God? Purity, the Fourth Ray, is the turning point on the spiritual path, the nexus of the figure-eight flow between the three first rays and the three upper rays. No one goes further on the path, no one goes beyond the first three rays, until they have mastered the initiations of purity.

What is the primary initiation? Some of you might, through previous dispensations, have come to see the Fourth Ray as that of the strict disciplinarians, such as Serapis Bey in his retreat at Luxor, who administers discipline—strict, unwavering discipline. The reality is that we of the Fourth Ray are one with the unconditional love of God. We are not disciplinarians in the sense that you see people on earth administer discipline, demanding blind obedience. We have, in fact, no desire whatsoever to have you blindly obey. We desire to see you be creative, but we, of course, desire to see you create in purity—in purity.

Pure intentions

How, then, do you begin to create in purity? Begin by considering your intent. What is your intent for creating? What is your motive? Is it pure?

What does it mean to be pure? What has been explained in the first messages from the first three rays is, of course, that the underlying creative force in the universe is the River of Life that desires all life to become *more* through constant self-transcendence. When your motive is pure, you desire both yourself and other people you encounter to be *more*.

Do you see the difference of how so many people on earth have been trapped by the impure beliefs and the impure feelings into not having the desire to raise up others? Instead, they have a desire to control others, to force them to fit into a certain matrix, into a certain mold—based on the underlying world view and belief system that forms the very core of their personal databases. These are the databases through which they look at and judge the world and other people and, of course, themselves. They think that they have to conform to this outer standard and that other people do as well. If other people will not do so, their negative feelings or their attempts to control others are justified. It is all for some greater good, whatever that good could possibly be when you consider that God has – over and over again – sent messengers to tell you to turn the other cheek, to resist not evil, to overcome your attachments.

How can you actually further the cause of God by seeking to force others? As has been explained, the ultimate vision of God is self-transcendence through free-will choices, whereby you become *more*. This is not because you are forced to, for you cannot be forced to be *more*. You can be forced to be less, you can be forced to be restricted or to restrict the creative flow through you, but you cannot be forced to be *more*. It must be a completely free-will choice where you desire to be *more*, you desire to let that creativity flow through you. Of course, how can you desire to be *more* for yourself? It cannot be done in a dualistic sense of seeking to raise the separate self. It can only be done in seeking to raise the greater self, the All.

Transcend miscommunication

This has led to innumerable impurities in peoples' view of each other, in peoples' tendency to judge one another. This has caused innumerable conflicts among human beings, innumerable misunderstandings, miscommunications. It has also caused the other form of miscommunication where people stop communicating because the impurities, that the two sides have in their databases, will not allow them to communicate and come to any kind of higher agreement or understanding, any sense of unity.

They will constantly speak past each other without ever reaching the heart, as you see outpictured between the Israelis and the Palestinians, even between the Pakistanis and the Indians. Of course, there are many other examples around the world, such as on the African continent where tribal warfare has now reached a crescendo. One must wonder when people will start questioning the basic paradigm behind the idea that our tribe is somehow superior to another, even though we all come from the same background, have the same genetic code, have the same outer looks, the same religion, the same nationality.

Impurities will make it impossible to communicate freely. Have we not said that true communication from the heart means coming into unity before you take any kind of action? Do you not see that precisely in the Middle East, they are not coming into unity? They are taking action based on the impure view and belief that they are separated, that they are in opposition to this other group of people.

You who are the wise ones, the more spiritual people, you have worked through the initiations of the first three rays during the reading of this book, as many of you have worked through them in your lives, even in past lives. You are now at the point where you face the initiations of the Fourth Ray, the initiations of purity. What has been attempted here is to take you to the point where you have had every opportunity to experience the unconditional love that we have for you.

Seeing all impurities

I wish you to look beyond any image you may have of the representatives of the Fourth Ray, such as the idea that we are disciplinarians or that we judge people. We do not judge anyone. We do see impurities and purities—we see the difference very clearly. No human being, no serpentine mind, can fool us into mistaking an impurity for a purity. It is simply not possible, for we are above the duality consciousness.

What we are here to help you achieve is a sense of co-measurement. Have we not explained the importance of the database that you have in your minds and how the analytical faculty of the mind will use such a database? Can you not see that your view of the world is colored by the database, and thus, of course, your view of purity and impurity is colored by the database? As I have explained, some people have come to believe that holding negative feelings or negative images of others is part of the work of their god and therefore in some sense must be pure.

The reality is that you cannot discern between purity and impurity by using the human intellect. Even if you were to study all of the spiritual teachings in the world and fill your subconscious database with their statements about what is pure and impure, you still would not be able to fully know – to fully experience – the difference between purity and impurity.

How can you come to know the difference? By encountering our Presence, our Purity in the Light, in the presence of which no impurity can hide, no impurity can disguise itself as purity. We are not here to judge you in any way, for you might think that we only see your impurities. This is not true, for we certainly also see the pure elements of your being.

I can tell you that there is not anyone who is serious about the spiritual path who does not have many purities in their beings, many pure images and views and understandings of the world, many pure feelings. This is known by people who have experienced some unconditionality, such as feeling happy, feeling gratitude, but a gratitude and a happiness that was not opposed by the dualistic opposite of ingratitude or unhappiness.

How purity is perverted

What the false teachers have attempted to use in order to trap the more spiritual people – those who have started to wake up – is that they have taken the pure qualities of God and they have attempted to turn them into dualistic qualities by defining what they think is an opposite. Of course, the purity of God is unconditional – is infinite – and thus cannot have an opposite.

Only in separation from Oneness can there be opposites. Only the duality consciousness can create opposites, meaning that when the forces of darkness create an imperfection – a perversion of a God quality – they are actually not creating an opposition or a perversion of the God quality—they are creating two qualities at once. They are creating the dualistic form of love and the dualistic form of anti-love. Those are the two qualities that oppose each other.

When people do not see this – do not see that even human love is impure – they are trapped in the eternal human struggle of seeking to cause human good – relative good, dualistic good – to win over dualistic evil. It cannot be done, my beloved.

Even if you think your intentions are pure and you are working for the cause of good or the cause of God – but you are seeking to fight other people who are evil – by the law of action and reaction, you create the opposite to your unbalanced action. You can never win that battle. There can never be peace on earth by killing other people. There can never be peace on earth by continuing conflict and holding impure feelings and impure images of other people.

Our offer to help you

You who are the spiritual people have begun to realize this, but many of you have so far only begun to understand it at a certain intellectual level and with some intuitive insights. What we offer you from the Fourth Ray is that we will manifest our Presence with you – as you are willing – and we will form that mirror of purity that will allow you to see both the purity and the impurity in your beings.

Some of you may have apprehension about this—being concerned that you might see so many impurities that you will be overwhelmed or ashamed or afraid that you will not be acceptable in the eyes of God. Then you need to study the teachings given earlier on the first three rays, and you will recognize that God does not condemn you. God only wants you to be free from the impurities, but God has complete respect for the Law of Free Will.

Those impurities have entered your being as a result of choices you made. Those choices were often not free choices because you were manipulated by the false teachers or by the state of affairs on planet earth where there is so much conflict. Nevertheless, you made the choice. The impurities can only leave your being when you make the choice to let them go, my beloved.

You can invoke the Violet Flame 24 hours a day for the rest of your lifetime – you can give rosaries, prayers, you can fast, you can do anything you can think of – but an impurity cannot be taken from you until you release it. You cannot release it until you see the original decision that caused you to allow it entry—and then undo that decision by replacing it with a pure choice, a choice based on the recognition of purity.

The catch-22

The goal of the false teachers is always to put you in a catch-22 from which you cannot move on, you cannot progress. Shame, guilt, fear are the very powerful tools that they use to create such a catch-22. They fool you into absorbing certain impure beliefs and generating impure feelings. Then they give you the further impure belief that what you have done is wrong and therefore God will condemn you for it—unless you seek to hide it. This mechanism prevents you from going through the process I have just explained of sensing the Presence of Purity, seeing freely the impurities, and freely letting them go.

There are other clever, subtle ways in which the false teachers have caused you to feel that you cannot let go or that you should not let go of these impurities, including, of course, the entire concept of the automatic outer path where you do not need to look at the beam in your own eye. You only need to declare Jesus Christ your Lord and Savior or get down on your knees five times a day and face Mecca, and then – "poof" – one day you will be saved. This is why people feel that they cannot – or they should not, or they will not, or they do not need to – take an objective look at themselves and experience the difference between purity and impurity.

Knowing that you are ready to take that step of taking an objective look at yourselves, I will then offer our assistance. I will offer to manifest my Presence with you, as does my consort Purity, as does Serapis Bey and all other representatives of the Fourth Ray—including Mother Mary who as the Mother of God is truly on all rays. She is beyond any ray, beyond the level of a chohan, beyond the level of an archangel, but has merged into the universal purity of that Mother of God.

Choose the master whom you want to manifest his or her Presence with you that you may have a sense of co-measurement of what impurity is holding you back from breaking through and having that turning point that Master MORE explained this book can be for you. We will offer to give you this as you sleep during the night, if you will ask to go to the retreat of Serapis Bey at Luxor.

There you will meet the master of your choice who will show you the impurity that blocks your breakthrough. He or she will also show you a pure aspect of your being that is the anti-thesis to that impurity, to that block, and thus enables you, empowers you, to overcome that block and rise above it.

You know you are *more* than that impurity and that no matter what might have happened in the past, nothing can stick to your immortal being. Nothing can stick to your conscious self, for you have the right "to be who you will be" and to decide at any moment to be *more* than those impurities and to step out of the identification with them. Let them go, I say, for I think you have had enough of them and you realize it is time to move beyond. This, then, is our gift, my beloved.

Beware of approaching the path intellectually

Some of you, in your eagerness to understand the path, have become a bit too intellectual. You have actually understood too much for your own good. You sometimes think that understanding is enough, but understanding alone cannot take you to the kingdom of heaven. You need all of the seven rays and even beyond to the eighth ray of Integration and beyond.

You cannot enter the kingdom of heaven by being strong on one ray and unbalanced on the others. It is only through balance – balance, of course, requiring purity – that you enter heaven. You cannot go on and attain true healing without first having encountered purity, the Presence of Purity.

What causes disease? Is it not impurities in the body? How can you be healed if you are not willing to see that the impurities in the body can only affect the cells if the cells respond to impurities in your consciousness? You realize that even though you might seek to cleanse and purify the body, it must start in the mind by you being willing to purify the subconscious database of these beliefs and feelings that you have thought you had to hold on to for fear of loss of identity.

[Breathes out]

I breathe out the pure love of the Fourth Ray. My beloved, understand that each of the seven rays is an expression of love with a coloring of the characteristics of the ray. Certainly, you can understand that the Fourth Ray of purity must have a pure expression of love, not the judgmental expression that you might think. We do not judge, for we see that any impurity in your being is temporary, is unreal. We see beyond it to the pure Being that you are, the pure Being that is an extension of the Creator's Being, that is an extension of the purity of your I AM Presence. It has an infinite potential to rise above any impurities that you might have taken in on your sojourn in this very dense sphere on this planet.

Know your pure identity

Many of you have volunteered to come here to raise up others. You have simply taken on a few impurities here and there that really have had no impact on the eternal part of your Being— and thus should have no impact on your sense of self. As you begin to encounter purity, you see just how impure and unreal and unimportant your ego is in comparison to your conscious self, which is always pure in the core of your Being. Your conscious self is the pure Being that says: "I AM." It is only at a lower level that you begin to say: "I am this. I am that."

At the level of I AM, no impurity can ever color your sense of identity. It is only when you begin to say: "I am this. I am that" that the impurities of this world can enter your container of self and color your sense of identity. That is when you can start the downward slide, but it has not affected the I AM of your Being. If you will be conscious of what you say about yourself – "I am this. I am that. I have this wound, I have that wound" – then you will be able to reconnect to the pure part of your Being, the I AM.

You will be willing and able to let go of the impurities—that are precisely the ghosts that Christ had to let go of on the cross. Indeed, you are going through these initiations, and you are all being used to teach each other and to bring out what needs to be brought out. Nothing is a matter of coincidence, for you have all volunteered to play certain roles in the play that we are enacting on earth. We seek to set the pattern of how spiritual movements can truly assist people in rising up through the levels of initiation, including purifying themselves of the imperfections that hold them trapped in a lesser sense of identity.

I, as have others, congratulate you for your willingness to play those roles, even if it has caused you in this lifetime to experience certain negative circumstances and take on what seems to be a heavy burden. When you reconnect to that I AM and realize you are *more* than the burdens – more than the wounds from childhood – suddenly, you gain a new vision, a new sense of co-measurement. How important are those old wounds really? How much hold do they have over the real you?

Ah, my beloved, there is no greater joy for us of the Fourth Ray than to see when people become aware of an impurity, see that it is not them, it is not part of their real beings. They joyfully let it go and walk into that freedom, that infinite joy of realizing that they are completely purified of that former condition, for it was unreal and temporary. They know now that they are real and they have an eternal part of their beings, and that is what they identify with. They know that those old impurities can never touch them again, for the prince of this world will come and have nothing in them, no impurity through which he can pull them into the old patterns of duality and struggle. This is our joy. This is our calling. This is our love. We are here to give you the fullness of that love, as you are ready to receive it. Determine how much you are willing to receive of the love of the Fourth Ray. I bid you goodnight, and I seal you in the pure Love of the Fourth Ray, the unconditional love of purity.

9 | I INVOKE
UNCONDITIONAL PURITY

In the name I AM THAT I AM, Jesus Christ, I call to my I AM Presence to flow through the I Will Be Presence that I AM and give this invocation with full power. I call to beloved Elohim Purity and Astrea, Archangel Gabriel and Hope, and Serapis Bey to help me overcome all blocks to my ability to communicate with pure intentions. Help me be free from all patterns or forces within or without that oppose my communication from the heart and my oneness with my I AM Presence, including . . .

[Make personal calls]

I. I am willing to see all impurities

1. I recognize that the weapon used by the false teachers is to expose me to impurities and perversions, and then get me to feel that I am obligated to take this in and hold on to it.

> Beloved Astrea, your heart is so true,
> your Circle and Sword of white and blue,
> cut all life free from dramas unwise,
> on wings of Purity our planet will rise.

> **Beloved Astrea, in God Purity,**
> **accelerate all of my life energy,**
> **raising my mind into true unity**
> **with the Masters of love in Infinity.**

2. I see that all spiritual teachers have always stated that in order to enter the kingdom of God, I must let go of all human impurities.

> Beloved Astrea, from Purity's Ray,
> send forth deliverance to all life today,
> acceleration to Purity, I AM now free
> from all that is less than love's Purity.

> **Beloved Astrea, in oneness with you,**
> **your circle and sword of electric blue,**
> **with Purity's Light cutting right through,**
> **raising within me all that is true.**

3. I recognize the two basic forms of impurity, namely the perversion of the father in the form of impure images, ideas, and beliefs. And the perversion of the mother in the form of impure feelings, impure energies.

> Beloved Astrea, accelerate us all,
> as for your deliverance I fervently call,
> set all life free from vision impure
> beyond fear and doubt, I AM rising for sure.

> **Beloved Astrea, I AM willing to see,**
> **all of the lies that keep me unfree,**
> **I AM rising beyond every impurity,**
> **with Purity's Light forever in me.**

4. I recognize that I have taken in impurities in the past. I also recognize that I did this as a result of choices I made. Therefore, I can let go of impurities by consciously changing the choices I made in the past. There is no impurity that I cannot transcend through this process.

> Beloved Astrea, accelerate life
> beyond all duality's struggle and strife,
> consume all division between God and man,
> accelerate fulfillment of God's perfect plan.

> **Beloved Astrea, I lovingly call,**
> **break down separation's invisible wall,**
> **I surrender all lies causing the fall,**
> **forever affirming the oneness of All.**

5. I hereby decide that I am willing to change. I am willing to come to see my impurities one by one. I am willing to surrender any impurity the moment I see it. I will lovingly let go of anything from the past.

> Beloved Astrea, your heart is so true,
> your Circle and Sword of white and blue,
> cut all life free from dramas unwise,
> on wings of Purity our planet will rise.

> **Beloved Astrea, in God Purity,**
> **accelerate all of my life energy,**
> **raising my mind into true unity**
> **with the Masters of love in Infinity.**

6. I realize that there is more to me than the impure self. I know that by letting go of impurities, I will not lose part of my identity. I will be reborn into a purer sense of self.

> Beloved Astrea, from Purity's Ray,
> send forth deliverance to all life today,
> acceleration to Purity, I AM now free
> from all that is less than love's Purity.

> **Beloved Astrea, in oneness with you,**
> **your circle and sword of electric blue,**
> **with Purity's Light cutting right through,**
> **raising within me all that is true.**

7. I am consciously surrendering the image of the angry, all-powerful God in the sky. I am attuning my being to the feminine aspect of God. I go into my heart and immerse myself in the flow of the River of Life.

> Beloved Astrea, accelerate us all,
> as for your deliverance I fervently call,
> set all life free from vision impure
> beyond fear and doubt, I AM rising for sure.

> **Beloved Astrea, I AM willing to see,**
> **all of the lies that keep me unfree,**
> **I AM rising beyond every impurity,**
> **with Purity's Light forever in me.**

8. I am willing to objectively, calmly look at myself and evaluate: "What is pure? What is impure in my consciousness?" I am willing to let go of all impurities in my forcefield, so that I can enter the kingdom of God.

> Beloved Astrea, accelerate life
> beyond all duality's struggle and strife,
> consume all division between God and man,
> accelerate fulfillment of God's perfect plan.

> **Beloved Astrea, I lovingly call,**
> **break down separation's invisible wall,**
> **I surrender all lies causing the fall,**
> **forever affirming the oneness of All.**

9. I am willing to go through the turning point on the spiritual path represented by the Fourth Ray. I am willing to go through the nexus of the figure-eight flow between the three first rays and the three upper rays. I am willing to master the initiations of purity.

> Accelerate into Purity, I AM real,
> Accelerate into Purity, all life heal,
> Accelerate into Purity, I AM MORE,
> Accelerate into Purity, all will soar.
>
> Accelerate into Purity! (3X)
> Beloved Elohim Astrea.
> Accelerate into Purity! (3X)
> Beloved Gabriel and Hope.
> Accelerate into Purity! (3X)
> Beloved Serapis Bey.
> Accelerate into Purity! (3X)
> Beloved I AM.

2. I will purify my intentions

1. I am willing to pass the primary initiation of the Fourth Ray. I am willing to transcend fear-based discipline and lock in to the unconditional aspect of purity, so that I can co-create in purity.

> Gabriel Archangel, your light I revere,
> immersed in your Presence, nothing I fear.
> A disciple of Christ, I do leave behind,
> the ego's desire for responding in kind.

> **Gabriel Archangel, of this I am sure,**
> **Gabriel Archangel, Christ light is the cure.**
> **Gabriel Archangel, intentions so pure,**
> **Gabriel Archangel, in you I'm secure.**

2. I am willing to purify my intentions. I am immersing myself in the River of Life that desires all life to become *more* through constant self-transcendence. I desire both myself and other people to be *more*.

> Gabriel Archangel, I fear not the light,
> in purifications' fire, I delight.
> With your hand in mine, each challenge I face,
> I follow the spiral to infinite grace.

> **Gabriel Archangel, of this I am sure,**
> **Gabriel Archangel, Christ light is the cure.**
> **Gabriel Archangel, intentions so pure,**
> **Gabriel Archangel, in you I'm secure.**

3. I am consciously surrendering all desires to control others, to force them to fit into a certain matrix, into a certain mold—based on the underlying world view and belief system that forms the core of my personal database.

> Gabriel Archangel, your fire burning white,
> ascending with you, out of the night.
> My ego has nowhere to run and to hide,
> in ascension's bright spiral, with you I abide.

> **Gabriel Archangel, of this I am sure,**
> **Gabriel Archangel, Christ light is the cure.**
> **Gabriel Archangel, intentions so pure,**
> **Gabriel Archangel, in you I'm secure.**

4. I am consciously surrendering the illusion that I can further the cause of God by seeking to force others. I accept that the ultimate vision of God is self-transcendence through free-will choices.

> Gabriel Archangel, your trumpet I hear,
> announcing the birth of Christ drawing near.
> In lightness of being, I now am reborn,
> rising with Christ on bright Easter morn.

> **Gabriel Archangel, of this I am sure,**
> **Gabriel Archangel, Christ light is the cure.**
> **Gabriel Archangel, intentions so pure,**
> **Gabriel Archangel, in you I'm secure.**

5. I make the completely free choice that I desire to be *more*, I desire to let infinite creativity flow through me. I desire to be *more* by seeking to raise the greater self, the All.

> Gabriel Archangel, your light I revere,
> immersed in your Presence, nothing I fear.
> A disciple of Christ, I do leave behind,
> the ego's desire for responding in kind.

> **Gabriel Archangel, of this I am sure,**
> **Gabriel Archangel, Christ light is the cure.**
> **Gabriel Archangel, intentions so pure,**
> **Gabriel Archangel, in you I'm secure.**

6. I am willing to experience the unconditional love that the masters of the Fourth Ray have for me. I ask you to help me achieve a sense of co-measurement and the ability to discern between purity and impurity by going beyond the human intellect.

> Gabriel Archangel, I fear not the light,
> in purifications' fire, I delight.
> With your hand in mine, each challenge I face,
> I follow the spiral to infinite grace.

> **Gabriel Archangel, of this I am sure,**
> **Gabriel Archangel, Christ light is the cure.**
> **Gabriel Archangel, intentions so pure,**
> **Gabriel Archangel, in you I'm secure.**

7. I desire to fully know and experience the difference between purity and impurity. I am willing to encounter the Presence of the masters of the Fourth Ray. I am willing to experience the Presence of Purity in which no impurity can hide, no impurity can disguise itself as purity.

> Gabriel Archangel, your fire burning white,
> ascending with you, out of the night.
> My ego has nowhere to run and to hide,
> in ascension's bright spiral, with you I abide.

> **Gabriel Archangel, of this I am sure,**
> **Gabriel Archangel, Christ light is the cure.**
> **Gabriel Archangel, intentions so pure,**
> **Gabriel Archangel, in you I'm secure.**

8. I am willing to see the pure elements of my own being, the pure images, the pure feelings. I am willing to experience unconditionality, the gratitude and happiness that is not opposed by the dualistic opposite of ingratitude or unhappiness.

> Gabriel Archangel, your trumpet I hear,
> announcing the birth of Christ drawing near.
> In lightness of being, I now am reborn,
> rising with Christ on bright Easter morn.

> **Gabriel Archangel, of this I am sure,**
> **Gabriel Archangel, Christ light is the cure.**
> **Gabriel Archangel, intentions so pure,**
> **Gabriel Archangel, in you I'm secure.**

9. I am willing to experience the purity of God that is unconditional – that is infinite – and thus cannot have an opposite.

With angels I soar,
as I reach for MORE.
The angels so real,
their love all will heal.
The angels bring peace,
all conflicts will cease.
With angels of light,
we soar to new height.

The rustling sound of angel wings,
what joy as even matter sings,
what joy as every atom rings,
in harmony with angel wings.

3. I will rise above the dualistic struggle

1. I see that only in separation from Oneness can there be opposites. I see that when the forces of darkness create a perversion of a God quality, they are creating two qualities at once. They are creating the dualistic form of love and the dualistic form of anti-love.

> Beloved Astrea, your heart is so true,
> your Circle and Sword of white and blue,
> cut all life free from dramas unwise,
> on wings of Purity our planet will rise.

> **Beloved Astrea, in God Purity,**
> **accelerate all of my life energy,**
> **raising my mind into true unity**
> **with the Masters of love in Infinity.**

2. I am consciously surrendering the eternal human struggle of seeking to cause human good – relative good, dualistic good – to win over dualistic evil.

> Beloved Astrea, from Purity's Ray,
> send forth deliverance to all life today,
> acceleration to Purity, I AM now free
> from all that is less than love's Purity.

> **Beloved Astrea, in oneness with you,**
> **your circle and sword of electric blue,**
> **with Purity's Light cutting right through,**
> **raising within me all that is true.**

3. I see that by seeking to fight other people, I am, by the law of action and reaction, creating the opposite to my unbalanced action. I am consciously surrendering the illusion that I can create peace by holding on to impure feelings and impure images of other people.

> Beloved Astrea, accelerate us all,
> as for your deliverance I fervently call,
> set all life free from vision impure
> beyond fear and doubt, I AM rising for sure.

> **Beloved Astrea, I AM willing to see,**
> **all of the lies that keep me unfree,**
> **I AM rising beyond every impurity,**
> **with Purity's Light forever in me.**

4. I am willing to have the masters of the Fourth Ray manifest their Presences with me. I ask you to form the mirror of purity that will allow me to see both the purity and the impurity in my being.

> Beloved Astrea, accelerate life
> beyond all duality's struggle and strife,
> consume all division between God and man,
> accelerate fulfillment of God's perfect plan.

> **Beloved Astrea, I lovingly call,**
> **break down separation's invisible wall,**
> **I surrender all lies causing the fall,**
> **forever affirming the oneness of All.**

5. I am consciously surrendering the fear that I might see so many impurities that I will be overwhelmed or feel that I am not acceptable in the eyes of God. I recognize that God does not condemn me, but only wants me to be free from all impurities.

Beloved Astrea, your heart is so true,
your Circle and Sword of white and blue,
cut all life free from dramas unwise,
on wings of Purity our planet will rise.

Beloved Astrea, in God Purity,
accelerate all of my life energy,
raising my mind into true unity
with the Masters of love in Infinity.

6. I recognize that all impurities have entered my being as a result of choices I made. Those choices were often not free choices because I was manipulated by the false teachers. I accept that because *I* made the choice, the impurities can only leave my being when *I* make the choice to let them go.

Beloved Astrea, from Purity's Ray,
send forth deliverance to all life today,
acceleration to Purity, I AM now free
from all that is less than love's Purity.

Beloved Astrea, in oneness with you,
your circle and sword of electric blue,
with Purity's Light cutting right through,
raising within me all that is true.

7. I acknowledge that an impurity cannot be taken from me until I release it. I cannot release it until I see the original decision that caused me to allow it entry. I am willing to undo all past decisions by replacing them with choices based on the recognition of purity.

Beloved Astrea, accelerate us all,
as for your deliverance I fervently call,
set all life free from vision impure
beyond fear and doubt, I AM rising for sure.

**Beloved Astrea, I AM willing to see,
all of the lies that keep me unfree,
I AM rising beyond every impurity,
with Purity's Light forever in me.**

8. I am consciously surrendering the illusion that God will condemn me for my wrong choices and that I need to hide them. I am willing to experience the Presence of Purity, seeing freely the impurities, and freely letting them go.

Beloved Astrea, accelerate life
beyond all duality's struggle and strife,
consume all division between God and man,
accelerate fulfillment of God's perfect plan.

**Beloved Astrea, I lovingly call,
break down separation's invisible wall,
I surrender all lies causing the fall,
forever affirming the oneness of All.**

9. I accept the Presences of Astrea and Purity, Serapis Bey and all other representatives of the Fourth Ray—including Mother Mary. I ask you to give me a sense of co-measurement of what impurity is holding me back from breaking through and having a turning point on my path.

> Accelerate into Purity, I AM real,
> Accelerate into Purity, all life heal,
> Accelerate into Purity, I AM MORE,
> Accelerate into Purity, all will soar.

> Accelerate into Purity! (3X)
> Beloved Elohim Astrea.
> Accelerate into Purity! (3X)
> Beloved Gabriel and Hope.
> Accelerate into Purity! (3X)
> Beloved Serapis Bey.
> Accelerate into Purity! (3X)
> Beloved I AM.

4. I am willing to have a breakthrough

1. I ask that during sleep I will be taken to the retreat of Serapis Bey at Luxor. I ask to meet the master who will show me the impurity that blocks my breakthrough. I ask to be shown the pure aspect of my being that is the anti-thesis to the impurity, and which empowers me to overcome the block.

Serapis Bey, what power lies,
behind your purifying eyes.
Serapis Bey, it is a treat,
to enter your sublime retreat.

O Holy Spirit, flow through me,
I am the open door for thee.
O mighty rushing stream of Light,
transcendence is my sacred right.

2. I acknowledge that no matter what might have happened in the past, nothing can stick to my immortal being. Nothing can stick to my Conscious You, for I have the right "to be who I will be." I hereby decide that I am *more* than all impurities, and I step out of identification with them.

Serapis Bey, what wisdom found,
your words are always most profound.
Serapis Bey, I tell you true,
my mind has room for naught but you.

O Holy Spirit, flow through me,
I am the open door for thee.
O mighty rushing stream of Light,
transcendence is my sacred right.

3. I consciously let go of all impurities. I have had enough of them and I realize it is time to move beyond. I am willing to achieve the balance that comes from encountering the Presence of Purity.

> Serapis Bey, what love beyond,
> my heart does leap, as I respond.
> Serapis Bey, your life a poem,
> that calls me to my starry home.

> **O Holy Spirit, flow through me,**
> **I am the open door for thee.**
> **O mighty rushing stream of Light,**
> **transcendence is my sacred right.**

4. I breathe in the pure love of the Fourth Ray. I see beyond all impurities to the pure Being that I AM, the pure Being that is an extension of the Creator's Being, that is an extension of the purity of my I AM Presence.

> Serapis Bey, your guidance sure,
> my base is clear and white and pure.
> Serapis Bey, no longer trapped,
> by soul in which my self was wrapped.

> **O Holy Spirit, flow through me,**
> **I am the open door for thee.**
> **O mighty rushing stream of Light,**
> **transcendence is my sacred right.**

5. I consciously acknowledge that I have an infinite potential to rise above any impurities that I might have taken in during my sojourn on this planet. The impurities I have taken on have had no impact on the eternal part of my Being—and thus will have no impact on my sense of self.

Serapis Bey, what healing balm,
in mind that is forever calm.
Serapis Bey, my thoughts are pure,
your discipline I shall endure.

O Holy Spirit, flow through me,
I am the open door for thee.
O mighty rushing stream of Light,
transcendence is my sacred right.

6. I am experiencing the Presence of Purity, and I see just how impure, unreal and unimportant my ego is in comparison to my conscious self. I AM always pure in the core of my Being. My Conscious You is the pure Being that says: "I AM." I will be conscious of what I say about myself using the words "I am."

Serapis Bey, what secret test,
for egos who want to be best.
Serapis Bey, expose in me,
all that is less than harmony.

O Holy Spirit, flow through me,
I am the open door for thee.
O mighty rushing stream of Light,
transcendence is my sacred right.

7. I reconnect to my I AM Presence, and I realize I am *more* than the role I have taken on here on earth. I see that this role is not the real me, and I joyfully let it go and walk into the freedom, the infinite joy of realizing that I am completely purified of that former condition.

> Serapis Bey, what moving sight,
> my self ascends to sacred height.
> Serapis Bey, forever free,
> in sacred synchronicity.

> **O Holy Spirit, flow through me,**
> **I am the open door for thee.**
> **O mighty rushing stream of Light,**
> **transcendence is my sacred right.**

8. I know that I am real and I have an eternal part of my being, and that is what I identify with. I know that those old impurities can never touch me again, for the prince of this world will come and have nothing in me, no impurity through which he can pull me into the old patterns of duality and struggle.

> Serapis Bey, you balance all,
> the seven rays upon my call.
> Serapis Bey, in space and time,
> the pyramid of self, I climb.

> **O Holy Spirit, flow through me,**
> **I am the open door for thee.**
> **O mighty rushing stream of Light,**
> **transcendence is my sacred right.**

9. I am receiving and accepting the fullness of the love of the masters of the Fourth Ray. I fully absorb the pure Love of the Fourth Ray, the unconditional love of purity.

Serapis Bey, your Presence here,
filling up my inner sphere.
Life is now a sacred flow,
God Purity I do bestow.

**O Holy Spirit, flow through me,
I am the open door for thee.
O mighty rushing stream of Light,
transcendence is my sacred right.**

Sealing:

In the name of the Divine Mother, I fully accept that the power of these calls is used to set free the Ma-ter light, so it can outpicture the perfect vision of Christ for my own life, for all people and for the planet. In the name I AM THAT I AM, it is done! Amen.

10 | COMMUNICATE THAT LIFE IS MORE

A dictation by Mother Mary, representing the Fifth Ray of healing and truth.

My Beloved hearts, I want you to see the evolution that I have gone through. As Mother Mary I am primarily known and revered by Catholics around the world. Although they sing the Ave Maria with great joy and great love in their hearts, they also put me in a neat little file folder in their Catholic databases. Yet, the word "Catholic" means universal, and I have ascended to the status of universality. This is also the initiation that you face as you ascend the spiral staircase of the spiritual path and pass from the initiations of the Fourth Ray into the initiations of the Fifth Ray of truth and healing.

Truth will not fit in your database

As Pontius asked when he was faced with the Living Christ in embodiment: "What is truth?" When you look at the earth, you will see that so many people, so many groups of people, have their individual databases. As has been explained, the very foundation for such a database is that you have a certain world view and belief system, you have certain paradigms that you consider to be absolutely true—and thus they are beyond questioning.

This means that when each of these groupings of people consider the question "What is truth," the topic, has already been colored by their basic world view. They are not open to any expression of truth that might upset the apple cart of them feeling that they have managed to force truth to fit in a nice file folder in their database—and therefore, they have their lives under some form of control.

The reality, of course, is that you are God-free spiritual beings, individual extensions of your Creator, co-creators with that Creator. This is the essence of the problem with the database: it imposes an image, a graven image, upon your identity. When the Conscious You accepts such an image, it also accepts the corresponding limitations to its self-expression on earth, thinking that its self-expression must fit into the mold and therefore there are certain expressions that are acceptable and some that are not acceptable. Meaning that suddenly the conscious self is no longer a co-creator who is allowing God's force of constant self-transcendence to flow through it. It has now become something less than the fully creative being it was designed to be by the Creator itself.

The illusion of lack

What happens when you accept this limited sense of identity is that you fall prey to the basic illusion of the false teachers, namely that this material world is separated from God's kingdom. Therefore, this material world is a world of limitations and lack. You can only get what you need for the separate self by taking it through force and control, taking it from those other people who are seeking to get it, to get that limited amount of abundance that you now think is all that there is.

Do you see why I had you give the *Nurturance Rosary* [See *www.transcendencetoolbox.com*] before this dictation? That rosary is specifically designed – in a very profound and holistic way – to challenge the illusion of lack, the illusion that you are not nurtured, that you are not fulfilled. The ultimate illusion of the false teachers is that when you live in a world that is separated from God, in a world that is limited, you must seek to find nurturance in this world.

Your being was not designed to seek nurturance in this world. Your being is designed to be a co-creator who has the River of Life flowing through you. In feeling that flow, you feel nurtured and fulfilled. It is the only way that you will ever feel nurtured and fulfilled. What shall it profit a man that he gains the whole world but loses the flow of God's creativity through his being? You might own the whole world but it will not satisfy your longing for *more*. You will only find fulfillment through oneness with the flow of God's creative force.

As we have said before, the price you pay, so to speak, of having free will is that you cannot stop making choices. Likewise the price you pay for being a co-creator is that if you stop creating, you will feel unfulfilled, unnurtured—you will feel empty.

Control means stopping creativity

You see the entire plot of the fallen beings who seek to control humankind? How can you control humankind? Only by seeking to stop creativity, for creativity is unpredictable. How do you attain control? Only if you can make everything predictable by making it mechanical—as opposed to creative.

So many of the philosophies and thought systems in this world have been designed specifically to cause the individual to shut off the creative flow through its being, thereby, of course, paying the price of feeling unfulfilled. Many are trapped into thinking that they can still find fulfillment by hoarding and possessing something from this world, or even by attaining fame or fortune or even by working for some greater cause.

Many have been fooled into believing that they should not seek fulfillment in this world, for this world is somehow sinful or lesser. No, they should work their whole lives – being satisfied with being dissatisfied – and then hoping for that ultimate fulfillment and satisfaction in the next world. Again, this is making sure that God's creativity cannot come in and overturn the tables of the moneychangers who have inserted themselves into the temples of people's very beings and cut off that flow of creativity. Instead, they are demanding that they be paid by people giving them their spiritual light.

Do you see that when Jesus overturned the tables of the moneychangers in the temple, it was a symbol for the living Christ coming into your being and overturning the tables of that which is untruth in your being and thus keeps you trapped? You are trapped because you do not dare to bring forth the creative solutions that can take you beyond any problem and any limitation you face in the material universe.

What is truth, my beloved? It is that the material world is entirely created from the energies of the Ma-ter light. The Ma-ter light – being spiritual – cannot be confined to the form that it has taken on. It can – at any moment – break the bonds of that form and transcend itself into a higher form. It will do so only when God's co-creators set it free from the old form, for it has vowed to maintain that form for as long as the people on this planet maintain their limited images in their databases—and then project a limited form onto the Ma-ter light through those limited images.

The force of liberation

What happens when you hold on to those images in the database and will not question them? There is a built-in force in the Ma-ter light that we have talked about as the second law of thermodynamics – as the force of Kali – that breaks down all imperfections. This is what the Hindus call "Shiva," the God of destruction, the destroyer of all that which has become, so to speak, set in stone and has taken on the form of a graven image, meaning any image that does not change.

That force itself will break down those towers of Babel that people have built – and that they think can reach into the heavens and that are not changeable or that could never fall apart – those institutions in finance that they think could never fail or should not be allowed to fail. They think that when the institutions are in danger of failing, the government should step in. I tell you, when the government does step in to prop up those institutions and prevent them from failing, there is a real possibility that the government will have to fail in order to set the people free from the illusion behind it.

There will always be that force of the Mother light – out of the unconditional love of God – that will not allow God's co-creators to be trapped forever in a limited sense of identity. It will come in and it will indeed overturn the moneychangers and their tables, overturn the illusions. It will upset the apple cart until the souls are free—free to bask in the light of creativity that is the very force of life itself. What God – you might ask logically – would allow his own co-creators to be forever trapped in that lesser sense of identity when he knows that they are so much more?

Disease is a message from life

This, my beloved, is what you need to realize on the Fifth Ray. You need to realize that if you insist on holding on to untruth, then that holding on to untruth will indeed cause what you so often call disease and other physical manifestations of imbalance. What is disease? It is a message from life itself that something has stopped the creative flow, some illusion has stopped the creative flow. If you want to overcome disease, there is only one way to do so and that is to reinstate – to reunite with – that creative flow so that you transcend the consciousness that causes the disease.

It is a common observation on earth that those who advance in years sometimes become set in their ways, as they say. The more set in your ways you are, the greater the possibility of a disease. There are many of you who have been spiritual people for all of your lives, possibly practicing various techniques that have been given by the ascended masters. You are advancing in years, you are feeling your bodies begin to manifest disease and you do not quite understand how this can be so when you have so diligently given the violet flame or other techniques for your entire life.

If you will be honest with yourselves and step back, you will see that in many cases it is because you have become set in your ways. You have actually allowed our spiritual teachings and our tools to reinforce your sense of rigidity, of living in a ritualized way. Every day you repeat the same ritual instead of allowing your intuitive faculties to give you daily directions and therefore be creative in your practice of any spiritual technique.

Even being creative in your studying spiritual teachings, allowing your own higher self – through the Key of Knowledge – to give you an understanding that is beyond the written word, beyond the spoken word, beyond what could possibly be expressed in words. Instead, experiencing the Spirit of Truth rather than a worded expression—which must of necessity be less than the fullness of the Spirit.

You are designed to be able to experience that fullness of the Spirit of Truth. If you believe that you need to settle for an expression in this world, you will limit truth. Truth will then challenge the images in your database that cause that limitation. How else can you be free? How else can you possibly be free to espouse – to accept, to co-create – a higher sense of identity?

Going beyond being a student

It is well and good to see yourself as a student on the spiritual path, but there comes a point when it is time to stop seeing yourself as a student and realizing that you have attained some level of mastery. Accepting that – and accepting that you have something to share with others, that you are now able to help others – this is the essence of the initiations of the Fifth Ray.

As you work your way up through the first three rays and enter into the Fourth Ray of beginning to see the impurities in your being, you will recognize that the essence of impurity in your being is the focus on the separate self. On the Fifth Ray you need to come to the point where you begin to seriously challenge and question the entire illusion that you are a separate being who is seeking to raise that separate being to some ultimate status where it becomes acceptable to God and thus is guaranteed to enter God's kingdom.

On the Fifth Ray you need to seriously begin to break down that sense of the separate self, that desire to raise the separate self. This is a delicate challenge. When you look at the world, you realize that the vast majority of the people are not walking the spiritual path in a conscious manner. They are so trapped in the mass consciousness that they are, so to speak, not truly individuals but are actually flowing along with the current in the collective consciousness. They do not have enough individuality.

In order to rise above that mass consciousness and truly make progress on the spiritual path, you need to have developed a certain amount of individuality, a certain sense that you are separate from the mass consciousness. Therefore, you can walk the spiritual path even though they continue to do their things and worshipping in regular churches or not being religious at all, instead focusing on an entirely materialistic lifestyle.

You need a certain strong sense of individuality in order to rise up through the initiations of the first four rays. Then – suddenly – that which has carried you up through the first four rays now needs to be challenged and questioned. You need to realize that the sense of individuality focused as a separate being cannot take you beyond the Fourth Ray. On the Fifth Ray you face the initiations of wholeness.

Wholeness and healing

Healing is wholeness, my beloved. What is it that keeps you out of wholeness? It is the illusions that focus on separation and lack. They are the ones, they are the illusions, that manifest as disease. How can you heal disease? Only by coming back into wholeness. How can you come back into wholeness? Only by overcoming the illusions of separation and lack that are the inevitable companions of that separate sense of self.

In order to come back into wholeness, you need to transcend the sense of separation. This does not mean that you lose your individuality. Instead of seeing yourself as an individual who is disconnected from God – from other people, from the world – you begin to see yourself as an individual who is connected to the whole, connected to your higher self, connected to the ascended masters, connected to the Creator itself. Through that connection, you are also connected to all life so that you might say with Christ: "Inasmuch as you have done it unto the least of these my little ones, you have done it unto me." Or "I, if I be lifted up, shall draw all men unto me."

There are so many people, even those who have been spiritual students for many years, who face the challenge of disease, and they seek to heal it by doing something to the separate self. They might take various courses, they might even work on their psychology, but what I am talking about here is the need to make a subtle shift in your self-perception. You do no seek to heal the separate self, you seek to lose the separate self and thereby merge into the true individuality that is an expression of the whole.

That is the way to heal disease. Any physical disease you see on earth is the outpicturing in matter of a particular state of consciousness, a particular illusion of the separate self. You can overcome the physical disease by getting to see the illusion and by truly letting go of it, by giving up the ghost, letting that separate self die.

The quest to perfect the separate self

There are millions of people in the spiritual or New Age movement who have attained some understanding of the spiritual side of life, but they are still trapped in thinking that they can somehow perfect the separate self. In their quest to make that separate self acceptable in the eyes of God, they pursue all manner of things, often seeking for some ultimate understanding, some ultimate ritual, some ultimate incantation, some ultimate scripture that will automatically give them access to the kingdom of God—make that separate self worthy. Thereby – without realizing it and with the best of intentions – they are seeking to take heaven by force. They are seeking to force their way into the wedding feast, where – as Jesus said 2,000 years ago – they will inevitably be exposed as not wearing the wedding garment.

The wedding garment is the seamless garment. What is the seamless garment? It is one that is whole because you do not see your individuality as being separated from other individual beings. You see it as being the facet of a greater whole, and you see others as being facets of that whole. What is the need for seams, for separation, for divisions when you no longer identify yourself based on the divisions found on this earth?

Communicating from wholeness

When you are asked: "Who are you, how do you see yourself?" you no longer say: "I am an American," "I am an Englishman," "I am a man," "I am a woman," "I am a Jew," "I am an Arab," "I am a Christian," "I am a Muslim." All of these divisions have faded away, for you see yourself as a co-creator only. As an expression of the Sun of God's Being, as a beam of sunlight, shining from the whole and illumining the world—but not alone. You are illumining the world together with all other sunbeams shining on this planet from the Creator's Being.

How can there be conflict when you see this truth? How indeed, my beloved? When you are in wholeness, you can never be in conflict with someone else, even if that person is not in wholeness. As has been explained by other masters, in wholeness you know the Law of Free Will. You can accept that other people are choosing to be in a lower state of consciousness that is not an expression of wholeness. You also know that this can never take you out of your wholeness. If you know that nothing in this world can take you out of wholeness, you cannot possibly feel threatened by anything in this world. You cannot be hurt by anything anyone will say. You can then enter communication with other people from a state of wholeness, rather than from a state of lack. Many people on this earth communicate with others from that state of lack, from that sense of being unwhole, of being unfulfilled, of needing something from this world, demanding something from this world. They think they have a right to demand from others, and therefore they blame others when they do not get what they think they are entitled to receive.

If you truly believe that you need something from another human being, then that shows that you have stepped outside of the wholeness of your own inner being. In wholeness you realize that the true source of nurturance, as is said in the rosary, comes through your own higher being, comes from the spiritual realm. As I said, you will only feel whole and fulfilled by experiencing the River of Life flowing through you.

You have no need for anything in this world, you are not here to get anything from others. You are here to give to others, to allow God to give to others through you. In *that*, you – as the individual who is not separated from the whole – find ultimate fulfillment. When you see yourself a part of the whole, you know that when you raise up another person, you are also raising up the whole, which is your greater sense of self, your whole sense of self.

Contentment versus fulfillment

Your communication then becomes entirely different. First of all, you are not vulnerable to other people's unbalanced communication – impure communication, untrue communication – where they so often lie to you in order to manipulate you. When you have gone through the initiations of the Fifth Ray – when you have gone through the initiations of the Fourth Ray, of separating purity from impurity, then ascending to the Fifth Ray of separating truth from untruth – you know that you can never be manipulated by anyone on earth.

You can see through their intent. Even if they believe it is pure, you see through it. You see how they are seeking to get something from you in order to reinforce their limited sense of self so that they can stay where they are, being content. You realize that this sense of being content in the material universe – and having turned the material universe into an end in itself – is one of the greatest traps that prevents people from rising on the spiritual path.

There are even people who are content in being unwhole. They have become so identified with a particular unbalanced expression – such as a particular race or religion or a personal viewpoint – that they simply will not let go of it. They are content to remain in it, but nevertheless their contentment will eventually be challenged by the force of Life that will seek to set them free—by them realizing that they desire *more*.

Contentment is not the same as fulfillment. There is fulfillment only in constant self-transcendence that is the ultimate expression of creativity where you are co-creating a new, greater identity every moment. You are not allowing yourself to remain trapped in the one that was sufficient for yesterday, for each day has its own expression. As Jesus said, you should be content with that, not always looking beyond. Nevertheless, you realize the ongoingness of life and that you cannot stand still even if you have been on the spiritual path for many years. You cannot allow yourself to feel that you know enough, you understand enough and what you are doing in a certain kind of practice or ritual is enough to get you to where you want to go.

The ongoingness of the River of Life means that nothing is ever enough. Yet in recognizing and tuning in to that reality

– that nothing is ever enough – you realize that everything is enough. There is fulfillment at every stage of the path.

The trap of the ultimate goal

Fulfillment comes from transcendence, not from ownership, not from possessing something that is static. This is another trap perpetrated by the false teachers, of making you pursue some ultimate goal and thinking that this will give you fulfillment. You need to find your fulfillment in self-transcendence and recognize that, right now, you are at a certain level. Fulfillment is in taking the next step to the level above you. You do not need to look at others and say: "Oh that person is so advanced spiritually, I can never be like that," or "I need to be like that before I am fulfilled."

Instead, you need to recognize that your fulfillment is found in transcending your current state, ascending to a higher state— not some ultimate state but a higher state. In *that* is your fulfillment. It is the ultimate fulfillment, my beloved. When you recognize that even the Creator is transcending itself, you recognize that there is no ultimate state. Your sense of self can be expanded indefinitely through creativity, which is not a finite force but an infinite force that has no limitations.

Be aware that the linear analytical mind, as has been explained, is designed to work with the world of form where everything is finite and thus has limitations. The truth is that you are not *of* the world—you are *in* the world. You came here from a realm that is beyond those limitations, and thus you are not bound by them. You can expand your sense of self beyond the level of limitations, beyond the level of the finite world.

Then you can *be* the fullness of the infinite Being out of which you are born and to which you can return in manifesting that fullness. You can even express a high degree of that fullness here on earth whereby you become the example for communicating to others that there is something beyond their current state, their current sense of identity. You become the living Christ who comes in to overturn the tables of the moneychangers in people's temples. The "moneychangers" representing the very illusion that they do not need to change, that they simply need to pay their dues and then everything will be taken care of, rather than going beyond the material world.

No finite requirement leads to infinity

The illusion of the material world is that you can somehow enter the spiritual realm and the kingdom of God by fulfilling a finite requirement. You cannot enter by perfecting that finite self so that it lives up to a finite requirement. You can enter only by letting the finite self die and returning to your infinite sense of identity. This is what so many people in traditional religions and in the New Age movement will not recognize. It is not a matter of perfecting the finite, it is a matter of transcending it by letting the old sense of self die.

Why do you no longer see yourself as a child? Why do you no longer identify yourself as a ten-year old, for example? Because the identity you had when you were ten has died. You, your conscious self, has been reborn into a higher sense of identity—at least if you did not have a childhood that caused you to be fragmented so that elements of that childhood identity are still in your being. Go with me as I explain the reality that no matter how difficult a childhood you may have had, you have already allowed many of these old separate identities to die—only you did not do it consciously.

What is the essence of the spiritual path, my beloved? Is it not that you become more aware, more awake? Did not the Buddha say: "I am awake," meaning he was aware of everything.

You cannot rise beyond a certain point on the spiritual path by letting the old identity die without being aware of it. There comes a point where you must be conscious of facing an old identity, looking it in the eye, realizing it is not the real you, deciding to let it die, to give up the ghost. You realize that you are crucified, your infinite spirit is crucified, by that finite sense of identity. You are willing to let it go in order to be resurrected, reborn into a more infinite sense of identity.

When you are willing to let the old sense of self die, you can rise to an entirely new level of communication from the heart. You are no longer seeking to communicate with others in order to either fill the lack in yourself or to protect your finite, separate self from being hurt. Instead, you are only seeking to give, you are only seeking to heal, you are only seeking to help other people come closer to wholeness, the wholeness that you now experience in knowing who you are.

Sound is a creative force

Look at the world, my beloved, and consider what I have said, namely that so many people are seeking for that ultimate way to secure something in the material world. Words – sound – are a creative force, as you see in Genesis: "And God said, 'Let there be light.'" God used words, used sound, to stir the Ma-ter light into manifesting a visible kind of light that could be molded into separate forms and that was set apart from the unmanifest void that Genesis calls darkness.

Sound is indeed a creative force, but so many people in this world – being trapped in the illusion that they need to find wholeness or nurturance in this world – are seeking for ways to use sound, to use the spoken word, to manipulate others. Some even seek to manipulate matter itself through various rituals and incantations where they seek to use sound to create a rhythmic force that can actually break apart matter itself and in some cases produce nothing of value other than giving these people a sense of having power over matter. They have come to crave this power because they have reached an almost ultimate state of separation, of thinking, as we have said, that this is their kingdom, that they own it, that God is not here and that they have a right to do with it whatever they want. This is the black magic of seeking to take heaven by force by using the creative force of sound to gain some kind of power over matter, even if it is a destructive power or a power that is aimed at gaining something – be it material things or life energy – for the separate self.

You who are the wise ones will, of course, realize that this is not for you. You are not seeking to use sound, including the spoken word, to force life or other people to give you what you think you need in a state of lack. When you pass the initiations of the Fifth Ray, you are not in a state of lack, and thus you realize you need nothing from this world. You also realize the reality of free will, and thus you are not seeking to use the creative force of sound in order to, so to speak, force the world to become better—even if it is for the greater good of the world. You recognize that the greater good of the world is that people are awakened through their free-will choices. You seek to use sound, you seek to use speech, in order to help people make the choice without forcing them to make the choice.

That is why you use spiritual techniques such as my invocations, to transmute the dense energies of the mass consciousness, thereby lifting people's burdens, lightening their burdens, until they are not so bogged down by the negative energy. They can begin to make more free choices where they realize that there is an alternative to responding in certain ways and being trapped in negativity.

You can also come to the point of using words in a way that seeks to uplift people, even challenge their illusions – as Jesus so often did with the scribes and Pharisees – in order to give them a choice between their database and a higher reality. These are all perfectly legitimate when they are done with a purity of motive that comes from the sense of wholeness. You are lifting up others, not by forcing them but by assisting them in making better choices whereby they come from within to the same realizations that you have come to. They choose *more* rather than less.

The immense power of surrender

I am not seeking to give you some outer rule for how you should communicate with others. When you rise above the initiations of the Fourth Ray, you rise above the level of consciousness where you need rules, outer rules, that you follow. You rise to the point where you need to begin to open yourself to the flow from your own higher being so that you are not acting based on some rule in your database. You are allowing the creative force of life itself to either bypass the database or you have purified the database of the imperfections – the matrices, perhaps even the valid matrices – of how the creative force should flow. You are allowing it to flow freely.

I have served for some time on the Fifth Ray of truth, and one of the concepts I have attempted to communicate to the world is the need to surrender, the power of surrender—the immense power of surrender. You may think that surrender is a passive activity, but it is not. It can indeed be an immense power. When you surrender the finite, you become empty, empty of finite matrices. In that emptiness, you become the open door for the infinite to find expression through you—without being hampered by those finite images in your database.

When you are truly empty through surrender, the greater power can flow through you, and it is greater than any power that can be attained through any of the forceful means that people have come up with. This is indeed why you saw that Moses had greater power than the black magicians in the Court of Pharaoh, that Jesus had greater power than the scribes and the Pharisees and the temple priests, or the demons who came to challenge him. It was not his power, it was a greater power of the flow of life itself that could flow through him because he had become empty. In being empty of the finite, he was being filled with the Infinite.

This does not mean that you become as nothing. It means that your individuality becomes empty of finite restrictions, and thus your true individuality can be expressed. There are those who think that Jesus was not an individual. Of course, it is not true. Jesus expressed Christhood through the prism of his individuality. Another might express Christhood in an entirely different way, as many people have indeed done without being recognized as such—partly because of the Christian illusion that there is one Christed being who could ever walk the earth. People fail to allow Jesus the victory that he expressed when he said: "Those that believe on me shall do the works that I did and even greater works." Surely, the desire of Jesus as a true teacher is to see his students surpass him in their expression of creativity.

The true works of Christ

Jesus desires nothing more than seeing you, who are his students in this day and age, surpass him in expressing creativity. This does not mean that you have to walk two miles on water whereas he walked one mile. It is an expression of creativity that is adapted to this day and age, which means letting your light shine, expressing truth in a way that people in the modern age can understand, can relate to, can be inspired by so that they are awakened to the possibility of being *more*.

This is truly doing the works of Christ. All those outer man-ifestations of the so-called miracles were not the greatest works of Christ. The greatest works of Christ was that he challenged people's sense of identity, challenged them to realize that there is more to being a self-aware being – even what they call a human being – than what most people had expressed at the time. I can assure you that no matter the fact that his teachings have been perverted, there is still an element of the mass consciousness that died after Jesus' mission. Before Jesus' mission, people's self-awareness was even more limited than what you see today.

I can assure you that the potential for a mass awakening to the spiritual reality simply was not there before Jesus walked the earth. People's sense of identity was restricted by the mass consciousness that Jesus challenged, and that literally was judged and taken from the earth after his crucifixion and resurrection. This has given all people on earth an entirely new opportunity that they did not know before Jesus came and had his victory on this earth.

Jesus and all of us want to see that momentum come to full fruition in this age where a critical mass of people go through that awakening, realizing who they are as spiritual beings, accepting it – accepting it, my beloved – and accepting that they have a right to express it. This is the message that you are here to communicate, that you volunteered to communicate. It will begin being communicated through you when you are willing to surrender—to be empty in a finite sense and be filled with the infinite Power, Wisdom, Love, Purity, Truth, Healing, Service, Peace, Freedom and all of the God qualities that you are an expression of through your individual God Flame.

What is truth? Truth is that you are more than human beings, that all people are more than human beings, that the earth is far more than a material, physical planet with limitations and disease and poverty. The truth is that nothing in the material universe is inevitable, nothing is unchangeable. Everything can be changed in the blinking of an eye of God when you realize that you are that eye, you are the hands and feet of God, you are the mouthpieces of God.

Come to that awakening! Allow yourself to go through that awakening so that you will never again look at yourself the old ways but realize you are *more*. At every moment, as you are becoming *more*, you are lifting up the entire planet. Through your collective efforts, there will be change, my beloved. There *will* be change, for there *is* change—for *you* are here.

Be sealed in the infinite joy of your spiritual Mother who rejoices in seeing your progress, who rejoices in seeing your willingness to overcome the past momentums, your willingness to be *more*. Be sealed in the infinite love of the Divine Mother, the love that is always *more* and that always sees you as *more*.

11 | I INVOKE
UNCONDITIONAL TRUTH

In the name I AM THAT I AM, Jesus Christ, I call to my I AM Presence to flow through the I Will Be Presence that I AM and give this invocation with full power. I call to beloved Elohim Cyclopea and Virginia, Archangel Raphael and Mother Mary, and Hilarion to help me overcome all blocks to my ability to communicate from wholeness. Help me be free from all patterns or forces within or without that oppose my communication from the heart and my oneness with my I AM Presence, including ...

[Make personal calls]

1. I challenge the illusions of matter

1. Mother Mary, help me ascend to the status of universality. I am willing to ascend the spiral staircase of the spiritual path and pass from the initiations of the Fourth Ray into the initiations of the Fifth Ray of truth and healing.

> Cyclopea so dear, the truth you reveal,
> the truth that duality's ailments will heal,
> your Emerald Light is like a great balm,
> my emotional body is perfectly calm.

> **Cyclopea so dear, in Emerald Sphere,**
> **to vision so clear I always adhere,**
> **in raising perception I shall persevere,**
> **as deep in my heart your truth I revere.**

2. I accept the reality that I am a God-free spiritual being, an individual extension of my Creator, a co-creator with my Creator. I will not allow my ego or the forces of darkness to project any graven image upon my identity.

> Cyclopea so dear, with you I unwind,
> all negative spirals clouding my mind,
> I know pure awareness is truly my core,
> the key to becoming the wide-open door.

> **Cyclopea so dear, clear my inner sight,**
> **empowered, I pierce the soul's fearful night,**
> **through veils of duality I now take flight,**
> **bathed in your penetrating Emerald Light.**

3. As the Conscious You, I accept no image that projects limitations on my self-expression on earth. I transcend the illusion that my self-expression must fit into a mold and that some expressions are acceptable and some are not acceptable. I am allowing God's force of constant self-transcendence to flow through me.

> Cyclopea so dear, life can only reflect,
> the images that my mind does project,
> the key to my healing is clearing the mind,
> from the images my ego is hiding behind.

> **Cyclopea so dear, I want to aim high,**
> **to your healing flame I ever draw nigh,**
> **I now see my life through your single eye,**
> **beyond all disease I AM ready to fly.**

4. I consciously reject the basic illusion of the false teachers, namely that this material world is separated from God's kingdom. I reject the idea that this material world is a world of limitations and lack. I reject the idea that I need to take something through force and control.

> Cyclopea so dear, your Emerald Flame,
> exposes every subtle, dualistic power game,
> including the game of wanting to say,
> that truth is defined in only one way.

> **Cyclopea so dear, I am feeling the flow,**
> **as your Living Truth upon me you bestow,**
> **I know truth transcends all systems below,**
> **immersed in your light, I continue to grow.**

5. I consciously reject the illusion of the false teachers, namely that because I live in a world that is separated from God, in a world that is limited, I must seek to find nurturance in this world.

> Cyclopea so dear, the truth you reveal,
> the truth that duality's ailments will heal,
> your Emerald Light is like a great balm,
> my emotional body is perfectly calm.

> **Cyclopea so dear, in Emerald Sphere,**
> **to vision so clear I always adhere,**
> **in raising perception I shall persevere,**
> **as deep in my heart your truth I revere.**

6. I accept that my Conscious You was not designed to seek nurturance in this world. I AM designed to be a co-creator who has the River of Life flowing through me. In feeling that flow, I feel nurtured and fulfilled.

> Cyclopea so dear, with you I unwind,
> all negative spirals clouding my mind,
> I know pure awareness is truly my core,
> the key to becoming the wide-open door.

> **Cyclopea so dear, clear my inner sight,**
> **empowered, I pierce the soul's fearful night,**
> **through veils of duality I now take flight,**
> **bathed in your penetrating Emerald Light.**

7. I consciously transcend the plot of the fallen beings who seek to control humankind. They are seeking to stop creativity, for creativity is unpredictable. I am consciously allowing the creative flow through my being, and I refuse to give my spiritual light to the forces that seek to restrict my creativity.

> Cyclopea so dear, life can only reflect,
> the images that my mind does project,
> the key to my healing is clearing the mind,
> from the images my ego is hiding behind.

> **Cyclopea so dear, I want to aim high,**
> **to your healing flame I ever draw nigh,**
> **I now see my life through your single eye,**
> **beyond all disease I AM ready to fly.**

8. I am hereby allowing the living Christ to come into my being and expose the untruth that keeps me trapped. I do indeed dare to bring forth the creative solutions that can take me beyond any problem and any limitation I face in the material universe.

> Cyclopea so dear, your Emerald Flame,
> exposes every subtle, dualistic power game,
> including the game of wanting to say,
> that truth is defined in only one way.

> **Cyclopea so dear, I am feeling the flow,**
> **as your Living Truth upon me you bestow,**
> **I know truth transcends all systems below,**
> **immersed in your light, I continue to grow.**

9. I consciously accept that the material world is entirely created from the energies of the Ma-ter light, which cannot be confined to the form it has taken on. As a conscious co-creator, I set the light free from the old form, and I project images from the mind of Christ, the mind of oneness.

> Accelerate into Wholeness, I AM real,
> Accelerate into Wholeness, all life heal,
> Accelerate into Wholeness, I AM MORE,
> Accelerate into Wholeness, all will soar.

> Accelerate into Wholeness! (3X)
> Beloved Cyclopea and Virginia.
> Accelerate into Wholeness! (3X)
> Beloved Raphael and Mary.
> Accelerate into Wholeness! (3X)
> Beloved Master Hilarion.
> Accelerate into Wholeness! (3X)
> Beloved I AM.

2. I communicate from wholeness

1. I recognize that disease is a message from life itself that something has stopped the creative flow through my being. I hereby reunite with that creative flow so that I transcend the consciousness that causes disease.

> Raphael Archangel, your light so intense,
> raise me beyond all human pretense.
> Mother Mary and you have a vision so bold,
> to see that our highest potential unfold.

> **Raphael Archangel, for vision I pray,**
> **Raphael Archangel, show me the way,**
> **Raphael Archangel, your emerald ray,**
> **Raphael Archangel, my life a new day.**

2. I am allowing my higher self and spiritual teachers to give me the inner directions as to what spiritual teachings to study, what techniques to practice and how to allow the creative flow through me. I am willing to experience the Spirit of Truth in its fullness.

> Raphael Archangel, in emerald sphere,
> to immaculate vision I always adhere.
> Mother Mary enfolds me in her sacred heart,
> from Mother's true love, I am never apart.

> **Raphael Archangel, for vision I pray,**
> **Raphael Archangel, show me the way,**
> **Raphael Archangel, your emerald ray,**
> **Raphael Archangel, my life a new day.**

3. I recognize that it is time to stop seeing myself as a student. I realize that I have attained some level of mastery. I accept that I have something to share with others, that I am able to help others. I realize that helping others is the essence of the initiations of the Fifth Ray.

> Raphael Archangel, all ailments you heal,
> each cell in my body in light now you seal.
> Mother Mary's immaculate concept I see,
> perfection of health is real now for me.

> **Raphael Archangel, for vision I pray,**
> **Raphael Archangel, show me the way,**
> **Raphael Archangel, your emerald ray,**
> **Raphael Archangel, my life a new day.**

4. I recognize that the essence of impurity in my being is the focus on the separate self. I challenge and question the illusion that I am a separate being. Beloved I AM Presence, help me break down the separate self and come back into wholeness.

> Raphael Archangel, your light is so real,
> the vision of Christ in me you reveal.
> Mother Mary now helps me to truly transcend,
> in emerald light with you I ascend.

> **Raphael Archangel, for vision I pray,**
> **Raphael Archangel, show me the way,**
> **Raphael Archangel, your emerald ray,**
> **Raphael Archangel, my life a new day.**

5. Beloved I AM Presence, help me shift my sense of identity, so I see myself as an individual who is connected to the whole, connected to my higher self, connected to the ascended masters, connected to the Creator itself. Through that connection, I am also connected to all life, and I say with Christ: "If I be lifted up, I shall draw all men unto me."

Raphael Archangel, your light so intense,
raise me beyond all human pretense.
Mother Mary and you have a vision so bold,
to see that our highest potential unfold.

Raphael Archangel, for vision I pray,
Raphael Archangel, show me the way,
Raphael Archangel, your emerald ray,
Raphael Archangel, my life a new day.

6. Beloved I AM Presence, help me make a subtle shift in my self-perception, so I do no seek to heal the separate self, but seek to lose the separate self. Help me merge into the true individuality that is an expression of the whole. Help me transcend the very consciousness that causes disease by seeing the illusion and truly letting go of it, giving up the ghost, letting that separate self die.

Raphael Archangel, in emerald sphere,
to immaculate vision I always adhere.
Mother Mary enfolds me in her sacred heart,
from Mother's true love, I am never apart.

Raphael Archangel, for vision I pray,
Raphael Archangel, show me the way,
Raphael Archangel, your emerald ray,
Raphael Archangel, my life a new day.

7. Beloved I AM Presence, help me weave the seamless garment that is whole because I do not see my individuality as being separated from other individual beings. I see it as being a facet of a greater whole, and I see others as being facets of that whole.

Raphael Archangel, all ailments you heal,
each cell in my body in light now you seal.
Mother Mary's immaculate concept I see,
perfection of health is real now for me.

Raphael Archangel, for vision I pray,
Raphael Archangel, show me the way,
Raphael Archangel, your emerald ray,
Raphael Archangel, my life a new day.

8. I no longer identify myself based on the divisions found on this earth. All divisions have faded away, for I see myself as a co-creator only. I AM an expression of the Sun of God's Being, a beam of sunlight, shining from the whole and illumining the world—but not alone. I AM illumining the world together with all other sunbeams shining on this planet from the Creator's Being.

Raphael Archangel, your light is so real,
the vision of Christ in me you reveal.
Mother Mary now helps me to truly transcend,
in emerald light with you I ascend.

Raphael Archangel, for vision I pray,
Raphael Archangel, show me the way,
Raphael Archangel, your emerald ray,
Raphael Archangel, my life a new day.

9. I now live the truth that other people can never take me out of my wholeness. I know that nothing in this world can take me out of wholeness, and thus I do not feel threatened by anything in this world. I cannot be hurt by anything anyone will say. I enter communication with other people from a state of wholeness.

With angels I soar,
as I reach for MORE.
The angels so real,
their love all will heal.
The angels bring peace,
all conflicts will cease.
With angels of light,
we soar to new height.

The rustling sound of angel wings,
what joy as even matter sings,
what joy as every atom rings,
in harmony with angel wings.

3. I find fulfillment in self-transcendence

1. I know I have no need for anything in this world. I am not here to get anything from others. I am here to give to others, to allow God to give to others through me. In that, I find ultimate fulfillment.

> Cyclopea so dear, the truth you reveal,
> the truth that duality's ailments will heal,
> your Emerald Light is like a great balm,
> my emotional body is perfectly calm.

> **Cyclopea so dear, in Emerald Sphere,**
> **to vision so clear I always adhere,**
> **in raising perception I shall persevere,**
> **as deep in my heart your truth I revere.**

2. I am willing to go through the initiations of the Fifth Ray of separating truth from untruth, and thus I know I can never be manipulated by anyone on earth. I cannot be manipulated by my ego into feeling content in the material universe, for I know the material universe is not an end in itself.

> Cyclopea so dear, with you I unwind,
> all negative spirals clouding my mind,
> I know pure awareness is truly my core,
> the key to becoming the wide-open door.

> **Cyclopea so dear, clear my inner sight,**
> **empowered, I pierce the soul's fearful night,**
> **through veils of duality I now take flight,**
> **bathed in your penetrating Emerald Light.**

3. I know there is fulfillment only in constant self-transcendence, which is the ultimate expression of creativity. I am co-creating a new, greater identity every moment. I never allow myself to be trapped in the identity that was sufficient for yesterday, for each day has its own expression.

Cyclopea so dear, life can only reflect,
the images that my mind does project,
the key to my healing is clearing the mind,
from the images my ego is hiding behind.

Cyclopea so dear, I want to aim high,
to your healing flame I ever draw nigh,
I now see my life through your single eye,
beyond all disease I AM ready to fly.

4. I am one with the ongoingness of the River of Life in which nothing is ever enough. In recognizing and tuning in to the reality that nothing is ever enough, I also realize that everything is enough. There is fulfillment at every stage of the path.

Cyclopea so dear, your Emerald Flame,
exposes every subtle, dualistic power game,
including the game of wanting to say,
that truth is defined in only one way.

Cyclopea so dear, I am feeling the flow,
as your Living Truth upon me you bestow,
I know truth transcends all systems below,
immersed in your light, I continue to grow.

5. I know that fulfillment comes from transcendence, not from possessing something that is static. I reject the illusion that the attainment of some ultimate goal will give me fulfillment. I find fulfillment in self-transcendence, in taking the next step on my path.

> Cyclopea so dear, the truth you reveal,
> the truth that duality's ailments will heal,
> your Emerald Light is like a great balm,
> my emotional body is perfectly calm.

> **Cyclopea so dear, in Emerald Sphere,**
> **to vision so clear I always adhere,**
> **in raising perception I shall persevere,**
> **as deep in my heart your truth I revere.**

6. I know I did not come from the world of form where everything is finite and has limitations. I came here from a realm that is beyond those limitations, and thus I am not bound by them. I expand my sense of self beyond the finite world. I AM the fullness of the infinite Being out of which I am born and to which I will return in manifesting that fullness.

> Cyclopea so dear, with you I unwind,
> all negative spirals clouding my mind,
> I know pure awareness is truly my core,
> the key to becoming the wide-open door.

> **Cyclopea so dear, clear my inner sight,**
> **empowered, I pierce the soul's fearful night,**
> **through veils of duality I now take flight,**
> **bathed in your penetrating Emerald Light.**

7. I am an example for communicating to others that there is something beyond their current state, their current sense of identity. I am the living Christ who comes in to overturn the tables of the moneychangers, the very illusion that they cannot or do not need to change.

> Cyclopea so dear, life can only reflect,
> the images that my mind does project,
> the key to my healing is clearing the mind,
> from the images my ego is hiding behind.

> **Cyclopea so dear, I want to aim high,**
> **to your healing flame I ever draw nigh,**
> **I now see my life through your single eye,**
> **beyond all disease I AM ready to fly.**

8. I am here to shatter the illusion that people can enter the spiritual realm and the kingdom of God by fulfilling finite requirements. I am here to demonstrate that we can enter only by letting the finite self die and returning to our infinite sense of identity.

> Cyclopea so dear, your Emerald Flame,
> exposes every subtle, dualistic power game,
> including the game of wanting to say,
> that truth is defined in only one way.

> **Cyclopea so dear, I am feeling the flow,**
> **as your Living Truth upon me you bestow,**
> **I know truth transcends all systems below,**
> **immersed in your light, I continue to grow.**

9. I say with the Buddha: "I am awake." I am willing to face my old identity, look it in the eye, realize it is not the real me, decide to let it die, and give up the ghost. I will no longer let my infinite spirit be crucified by that finite sense of identity. I am letting it go and I am reborn into a more infinite sense of identity.

Accelerate into Wholeness, I AM real,
Accelerate into Wholeness, all life heal,
Accelerate into Wholeness, I AM MORE,
Accelerate into Wholeness, all will soar.

Accelerate into Wholeness! (3X)
Beloved Cyclopea and Virginia.
Accelerate into Wholeness! (3X)
Beloved Raphael and Mary.
Accelerate into Wholeness! (3X)
Beloved Master Hilarion.
Accelerate into Wholeness! (3X)
Beloved I AM.

4. I surrender all that is finite

1. I am rising to an entirely new level of communication from the heart. I am seeking to communicate with others in order to give, to heal, to help other people come closer to wholeness, the wholeness that I now experience in knowing who I AM.

> Hilarion, on emerald shore,
> I'm free from all that's gone before.
> Hilarion, I let all go,
> that keeps me out of sacred flow.

O Holy Spirit, flow through me,
I am the open door for thee.
O mighty rushing stream of Light,
transcendence is my sacred right.

2. I am seeking to use the creative force of sound in order to awaken people through their free-will choices. I seek to use speech in order to help people make better choices without forcing them. I am open to the flow from my I AM Presence, and I am allowing it to flow freely.

> Hilarion, the secret key,
> is wisdom's own reality.
> Hilarion, all life is healed,
> the ego's face no more concealed.

O Holy Spirit, flow through me,
I am the open door for thee.
O mighty rushing stream of Light,
transcendence is my sacred right.

3. In oneness with Mother Mary, I recognize the need to surrender. I recognize the immense power of surrender. I surrender the finite, and I am empty of finite matrices. In that emptiness, I am the open door for the infinite to find expression through me.

Hilarion, your love for life,
helps me surrender inner strife.
Hilarion, your loving words,
thrill my heart like song of birds.

O Holy Spirit, flow through me,
I am the open door for thee.
O mighty rushing stream of Light,
transcendence is my sacred right.

4. I surrender all finite restrictions so that my infinite individuality can be expressed. I am expressing Christhood through the prism of my individuality. I will give Jesus his victory by allowing my I AM Presence to do greater works through me than were done through Jesus.

Hilarion, invoke the light,
your sacred formulas recite.
Hilarion, your secret tone,
philosopher's most sacred stone.

O Holy Spirit, flow through me,
I am the open door for thee.
O mighty rushing stream of Light,
transcendence is my sacred right.

5. In oneness with Jesus, I allow the expression of creativity that is adapted to this day and age. I am challenging people's sense of identity, challenging them to realize that there is more to being human than what most people can imagine.

> Hilarion, with love you greet,
> me in your temple over Crete.
> Hilarion, your emerald light,
> my third eye sees with Christic sight.

> **O Holy Spirit, flow through me,**
> **I am the open door for thee.**
> **O mighty rushing stream of Light,**
> **transcendence is my sacred right.**

6. In oneness with Jesus, I fully accept that I am a spiritual being. I accept that I have a right to express my infinite self in this world. I surrender, and I am empty in a finite sense. I am filled with the infinite Power, Wisdom, Love, Purity, Truth, Healing, Service, Peace, Freedom and all of the God qualities of my individual God Flame.

> Hilarion, you give me fruit,
> of truth that is so absolute.
> Hilarion, all stress decrease,
> as my ambitions I release.

> **O Holy Spirit, flow through me,**
> **I am the open door for thee.**
> **O mighty rushing stream of Light,**
> **transcendence is my sacred right.**

7. I fully accept that I am more than a human being, that the earth is more than a material, physical planet with limitations and lack. I accept that nothing in the material universe is inevitable, nothing is unchangeable. Everything can be changed in the blinking of an eye of God, for I accept that I am that eye, I am the hands and feet of God, I am the mouthpiece of God.

> Hilarion, my chakras clear,
> as I let go of subtlest fear.
> Hilarion, I am sincere,
> as freedom's truth I do revere.

> **O Holy Spirit, flow through me,**
> **I am the open door for thee.**
> **O mighty rushing stream of Light,**
> **transcendence is my sacred right.**

8. I am awakening! I am allowing myself to go through that awakening, and I will never again look at myself the old ways. I realize that I AM *more*. At every moment, as I am becoming *more*, I am lifting up the entire planet. I accept that there will be change, that there *is* change, for I AM here.

> Hilarion, you balance all,
> the seven rays upon my call.
> Hilarion, you keep me true,
> as I remain all one with you.

> **O Holy Spirit, flow through me,**
> **I am the open door for thee.**
> **O mighty rushing stream of Light,**
> **transcendence is my sacred right.**

9. I accept that I am sealed in the infinite joy of my spiritual Mother who rejoices in seeing my progress, who rejoices in seeing my willingness to overcome the past momentums, my willingness to be *more*. I am sealed in the infinite love of the Divine Mother, the love that is always *more* and that always sees me as *more*.

Hilarion, your Presence here,
filling up my inner sphere.
Life is now a sacred flow,
God Vision I on all bestow.

O Holy Spirit, flow through me,
I am the open door for thee.
O mighty rushing stream of Light,
transcendence is my sacred right.

Sealing:

In the name of the Divine Mother, I fully accept that the power of these calls is used to set free the Ma-ter light, so it can outpicture the perfect vision of Christ for my own life, for all people and for the planet. In the name I AM THAT I AM, it is done! Amen.

12 | SERVE FULLY BY BEING AT PEACE

A dictation by Jesus, representing the Sixth Ray of peace and service.

I AM the Real Jesus—not the fake Jesus that people have been worshiping for nigh 2,000 years, thinking that I need to be worshiped by human beings. Nay, why would I need to be worshiped when I AM indeed an expression of the God Flame of unconditional, infinite, never-ending, inexhaustible Joy?

Now, how many of you – most of you having grown up in a Christian culture – would associate joy with the name "Jesus Christ?" Apparently, none of you! And it is quite understandable, my beloved, for I dare say that if you were to ask that question of the billions of Christians on this earth, few of them would dare to answer in the affirmative.

The stigma created by the perverted Christianity over these 2,000 years hangs over this planet like a dark cloud. Yet I must tell you that I came with a joyful message. As my Mother, both physical and spiritual, said yesterday, there was a certain consciousness of death that was judged and taken from this planet as a result of my victory and resurrection. It was indeed a very joyous and joyful event, setting people free, giving them the potential to rise to a higher level of consciousness.

I come to bring joy to the world

I come today to bring more of that Joy Flame so that those who are willing – those who are prepared at inner levels, some during many embodiments over these past 2,000 years of seeing every shading of Christianity – can accept, indeed, the joyful message of my coming. The kingdom of God is at hand!

When that death consciousness was lifted, it did indeed become possible for many people to embody the Christ consciousness on earth, which had not been – in practicality – possible before although it was possible in theory. It was possible for a few, but certainly not possible for the many. We have now the unprecedented potential that many people can dare to embody Christhood and dare to express it, dare to communicate it to the world.

The essential service

As a representative of the Sixth Ray of God Peace and God Service, let me expound on how that ray can help you communicate from the heart. The essence of service is what? It is precisely, as other masters have spoken about, that you come to the realization that all life is One and that the only way to raise up yourself is to raise up the All.

As I said 2,000 years ago: "Greater love has no man than to lay down his life for a friend." Greater love has no spiritual being in heaven than to lay down that spiritual life, enter into the material realm that is dominated by the death consciousness in order to awaken a friend to the potential to rise above that consciousness. My embodiment as Jesus exemplified that which in the East is called the Bodhisattva vow. Those who hear the cries of the world, and instead of leaving the world behind stay with it – often re-embodying in it although they have no karmic reason for doing so – in order to help their unascended brothers and sisters awaken to their higher potential.

When you have passed the initiations of the Fifth Ray, this becomes the very foundation for communication from the heart: the desire to serve and to raise all life. Here we must take a look at how this concept of service can be perverted—and has been perverted by those who are trapped in the illusion of the separate self. They are betrayed by their own good intentions into thinking that in order to serve other people, it is acceptable to force them – somehow – to be saved by becoming members of a particular religion that they have come to believe will give them automatic entry into the kingdom of heaven. I made many statements and gave several parables specifically to show you that no outer religion can guarantee your entry to the wedding feast, for the kingdom of God is within. How can you enter that inner kingdom through any external means, my beloved?

It can only happen through a transformation of consciousness, a transformation of the heart. You cannot force anyone to go through that transformation. It must come from within the being as the result of free choices.

Show people that there is more

What you can do is show them that they have hope. They have hope that there is a better life and that they can attain it, if they are willing to look for it. You can go and bring that hope by demonstrating that there is a higher state of consciousness where you are not afraid to stand in front of the high and the

234   🔅   How to Communicate from the Heart

mighty of this world—the power elite of this world, the temple priests and the scribes and the Pharisees in both the fields of science and religion. You are not afraid to stand before them and give witness to your spiritual – not beliefs – your spiritual knowledge, your spiritual being, your God realization. For you God is not a theoretical concept that one can argue for or against endlessly without coming up with a final answer. You have the final answer in experiencing the Living God within you.

"I and my Father are One." This was my statement of joy. It was the proof that there is a God, the only proof that can ever be when you consider free will. There cannot be an ultimate argument. There cannot be some manifestation in the heavens that all can see and none can deny, for it would violate the very Law of Free Will itself. Understand that even my miracles – my so-called miracles – were only shown to a few at the time and were actually not meant to be used to set me apart from other human beings, turning me into some kind of a god, or rather a false god, for there is none good but God, so why callest thou me good? Why callest thou me god when I myself said: "I can of my own self do nothing?" How can you then come out and claim that Jesus Christ was God from the very beginning and that he had never sinned and that he could never have failed in his mission? What nonsense is this! I look to you to not be afraid to challenge this, but indeed to challenge it at every opportunity, my beloved.

Question the unquestionable

One of the greatest plots of the false teachers is to create an environment where none dare to speak out about the underlying paradigms and assumptions that they have elevated to the status of infallibility. Think about what other masters have said about the database in the subconscious mind and how it is founded upon a particular world view. The false teachers have attempted to pull everyone into accepting one of the dualistic belief systems as the foundation for their personal database. They attempt to create an environment where no one dares to speak out and challenge those dualistic illusions.

As long as those dualistic illusions are not challenged, the people look at every aspect of life through the filter of those illusions, having built their personal databases entirely on those illusions. How can they ever come to see the living truth? How can they come to experience the Spirit of Truth, which cannot – certainly, you can see – be fit into any database based on duality? This is the catch-22 where the false teachers, the blind leaders, seek to hold people indefinitely, thinking that if they can hold people trapped, they can maintain control over this planet. They are not able to realize that the very force of the Mother Kali will break down all of their prison walls.

As my Mother explained, you cannot be satisfied, fully satisfied, by anything in this world. Even if you have a beautiful theological foundation that describes God and the heaven world and the road to salvation, you still cannot be fully satisfied with it. Even the teachings we have given in this day and age, teachings that are way beyond the old dogmas and doctrines, teachings that I have put on my website and that are available elsewhere, those teachings by themselves cannot satisfy you fully. You desire to go beyond an outer teaching expressed in words and experience the Living God, the Spirit of Truth within you.

Is objectivity possible?

This desire is the hope for the awakening of humankind—when you dare to witness that you had that desire, that you were willing to follow it and that you have indeed experienced the Living God. Those trapped in the duality consciousness seek to deny or ridicule every aspect of this experience, seeking to come up with a very "clever" belief that everything is just a matter of subjective experience, that there is no objective experience, no objective reality.

Understand the subtle difference. You are an individualization of the Creator's Being. The Creator is omnipresent. Your sense of self is focused at a particular localized point. The Creator sees everything from the omnipresent perspective; you see the world from your localized perspective. Do you see that, certainly, you do not have the omnipresent perspective of the Creator? Does that mean you cannot have an objective experience?

Well, that depends on how you define "objective." If the materialists are right that you cannot have an objective experience, then they have nullified their own philosophy and argument. Because it follows logically that materialism and their belief in materialism – and their belief in the superiority of materialism over any form of faith – is also their subjective experience. They cannot be any more right than any religion. They are in fact arguing that: "My subjective experience is superior to your subjective experience." This of course – if they were honest – nullifies their entire argument.

We come to the realization that we need a slightly deeper understanding of the concept of objectivity, and it is very simple. As we have said, any human being on this planet is at this very moment looking at the world through his or her personal database. It forms a filter for how you look at everything, how you categorize any experience by relating it to your previous experiences and beliefs in the database. Seeing the world through the filter of your database is a subjective experience. Whether you are a religious person who believes in God – but has never experienced the Presence of God – or whether you are a materialist who denies the existence of God, you are seeing the world through your subjective filter. It is indeed possible for human beings to come to see one or a few steps beyond their present filter, to expand their database, or even to go beyond the database and experience a new understanding, a higher understanding.

Science and objectivity

For centuries science has precisely empowered people to see beyond some of the hypocrisy and superstition created by the rigid Christianity of the Middle Ages. Do you not see that science itself claims that it is possible to have an objective experience? What scientists are currently denying is that one can have such an experience through consciousness.

As quantum physics has proven, you can never have an experience that is not coming through your consciousness. The question of how objective your experience is depends on how dense the filter of your personal database is. When you go through a conscious effort of questioning and challenging the assumptions and beliefs in your database – replacing them with a higher understanding, or perhaps discarding them altogether – you can gradually work towards a state of consciousness where even though you still see the world from a localized perspective, you are not seeing the world through the filter of a database filled with dualistic beliefs. This, my beloved, is the true definition of objectivity.

This does not mean that there is some ultimate standard of objectivity that you can attain while still in embodiment. The only ultimate standard of objectivity is the omnipresent awareness of the Creator. Nevertheless, it means that those who are willing to see beyond duality – those who are willing to consider how their view of the world is colored by their database – can work towards a state of mind where they are clear from the dualistic beliefs. Instead of seeing through a glass darkly, as Paul expressed it, they can now see him for who he is. They can see Christ reality. They can see themselves as spiritual beings, extensions of the Creator's Infinite Being, focused in a particular point in the finite world, but with an infinite potential to go beyond it and embrace infinity.

Overcoming death

These are important concepts to communicate to people in this day and age. We of the ascended masters did indeed sponsor science as the only way to help humankind rise above the superstition of the Dark Ages. We knew the very real potential that humankind would swing into the other extreme and deny any kind of faith or see it as superstition, wanting instead to only trust what they could see through their senses or material instruments. Thereby, of course, they confine themselves to a world view that is limited by the material world itself, making the material world a self-contained sphere from which there seems to be no escape.

If there is nothing beyond the material world, then what is the hope of ever escaping mortality, of ever escaping the consciousness of death? If you have no hope of escaping death, how can you escape the fear of death? You will inevitably be controlled by that fear, as most people are today in this world.

Oh death, where is thy victory, for death has lost its sting. This is my desire, having come into this world and demonstrated that you can go through physical death but continue an existence through the resurrection to your true spiritual identity. I desire all people to go through that transformation of coming from death into life, from the death consciousness into the life consciousness. This is the message that I desire to see communicated and spoken from the heart—not from an intellectual understanding. You cannot make someone understand this intellectually, precisely because of what we have explained about the database.

When the person sees the world through the filter of an intellectual database based on the consciousness of materialism, the person will never be able to see the logic in something beyond. The person must have an experience of something beyond, and the person might be inspired to open his or her mind to such an experience by seeing you demonstrate it. Not in the rigid, dogmatic, fanatical way that so many still preach religion in this world, thinking they can actually scare people into being converted. So few people in today's world can actually be scared into a conversion, although there are certainly some left at that level of consciousness. Nay, your role is to preach to those who are ready to go beyond fear and find an approach to spirituality that is not based on fear.

Speaking without fear

How can you communicate such a spiritual message? Only when you speak from the heart, for only then will you speak without fear. Of course, you must then come to a point where you have attained non-attachment to other people's reactions.

Why is the Sixth Ray the ray of service *and* peace? It is simply because you cannot give true service to life unless you are fully at peace. Only when you are at peace, can you remain centered in the heart no matter what other people send at you. Only then can you speak from the heart. Only when you speak from the heart, can you shock people out of their present state of consciousness and demonstrate to them that there is real hope of rising above that state of consciousness.

When you respond in kind when people are unkind to you, you only affirm to them their subtle belief – often unconscious – that the world is a negative place filled with negative people. How will they then escape negativity, no matter how well you might argue at the intellectual level? You must show them unconditional love by turning the other cheek. Whereby I mean you do not respond by speaking to them with the same vibration that they speak to you—even if they seek to ridicule your beliefs or yourself or your very life.

If you respond in kind or if you become defensive, you only confirm to them that there is nothing beyond that state of the dualistic struggle. When you turn the other cheek by not responding in kind – by speaking from the heart, whatever that entails, be it tough love or gentle love – you shock them into thinking. When they start thinking, there is the real possibility that they will realize there is something beyond.

Maybe it takes many demonstrations, many encounters with you and other people who are speaking from the heart. There are very, very, very few people on this planet who could not be touched by continually encountering people who speak from the heart. You do not need to worry about the people who cannot be touched, for the law of God and the angels of Archangel Michael will take care of them in due time. They will take them to a place where they might receive a different kind of opportunity than they have received on this planet so that they will not weigh down the planet. Indeed, you will bring about the judgment of these souls if you let them rail against you and persecute you for my sake.

Speak from a state of peace

Do you see how – in order to speak from the heart, and continue to speak from the heart – you must be at peace? You can be at peace only when you are non-attached to other people's reactions and responses. That non-attachment I demonstrated by speaking out in front of the high and the mighty and the low and the humble of my time, and letting them do whatever they wished to do with me, even nail me to that cross and kill my physical body. Did I not demonstrate that non-attachment by saying: "Father forgive them, for they know not what they do." You can come to that point yourself, that point of inner peace, of knowing that whatever people to do you, you will simply be non-attached; you will ask God to forgive them. You will give up any ghost – the ghost represented by their consciousness – and rise above it. You will not allow them to prevent your self-tran-scendence into ever higher levels of Christ consciousness.

Do you see, when you look at my life as Jesus, that I spoke in many different ways? Sometimes I spoke softly and gently. Sometimes I was challenging and in people's faces, as they say. Other times I spoke as you hear me speak now: "For he spoke not as the scribes; he spoke with authority."

I will suggest that you first practice speaking gently. I strongly suggest that you do not limit yourself – or rather your higher being expressing itself through you – to always speaking gently. Instead, you work on coming to the point where you are so non-attached that you can let your higher being speak through you in any way the situation warrants. You do not ana-lyze with the outer mind what to say or how to say it to a certain person, but you do as Mother Mary explained. You surrender; you empty yourself—and you let the Spirit fill you. Did I not say to my disciples: "Take no thought for what ye shall say, it shall be given unto you." When you come to that point, my beloved, then the Spirit will speak through you.

How do you know when the Spirit is speaking?

The question, of course, that many of you are asking yourselves is: "Well how do I get to that point? How do I know when it is the Spirit speaking through me and when it is not?"

Here is the simple equation that so many people have failed to understand. You get to the point where the Spirit will always speak through you by being willing to speak out, even if you are wrong or not at the highest vibration. There are two kinds of students that we, as spiritual teachers, face. There are those who say: "Oh Lord, I will do anything you ask—when I have become perfect and cannot make a mistake. So you, Lord, should take me to that point of perfection, and then I will do anything you ask."

It cannot be done that way. How do you attain mastery? As the old saying goes: "Practice makes perfect." If you are not willing to practice, you cannot learn. If you are not willing to speak out based on the understanding and the attainment you have today, you are not multiplying your talents, are you? If you are not multiplying your talents, you will not rise to a higher level of consciousness, and thus you cannot receive *more* from the Spirit.

Those who are the best servants are not those who work for perfection. They are the other kind of students who say: "I am willing to multiply what you have given me thus far. I am willing to speak out based on my understanding. It may be hurtful. I may be ridiculed by others. I may even come to the realization that I have been naive or had a partial understanding." You may feel that: "I have been wrong so many times in speaking out." Yet you have a right to speak out at your present level of awareness and understanding—and then learn from that, because that is the way to progress faster on the path.

No progress without experimentation

As a scientist you can conduct an experiment. If you are trying to make a light bulb, the experiment might turn out that you create the light bulb or it might turn out that you do not. Either way you make progress because now you know which will work and now you know which will not work. That enables you to move on and try other materials that might work until you find the right one. How can you as a scientist make any kind of progress if you refuse to have "failed" experiments?

If you seek knowledge and understanding until you feel you know everything and can never make a mistake, the world might just have ascended before you are ready to speak out. The world will not wait until you have overcome your fears of speaking out.

That is why I walked up to my disciples 2,000 years ago and said: "Leave your nets and follow me." If they did not follow me, they were left behind, entangled in those nets. The greatest mistake – if you want to talk in terms of mistakes – that you can make – one might even say the *only* mistake you can make – is not to dare to experiment, not to dare to speak out.

When souls pass from the screen of life and into the spiritual realm and meet their spiritual teachers and have a life review of what they accomplished or did not accomplish in their latest embodiment, the universal, greatest regret that people have is what they did not do, did not say, what they left undone, what they left unsaid. It is not the mistakes they made; it is the opportunities that were lost because they were too afraid to act or speak. That is why I told my disciples not to hide their light but to shout it from the housetops.

You must TRY

This messenger has grown immensely in the last few years where he has been doing the Ask Real Jesus website. This implies that he was far from perfect when he started it and is certainly not perfect now. By being willing – even though he was aware of certain imperfections – to still put himself out there, he has learned more than he could ever have learned by staying in his little comfortable sphere and studying until he had reached some state of "perfection." You all know this because you all learned to ride a bicycle. You did not learn it by watching a video on

How to Communicate from the Heart

YouTube or reading the instruction manual. You only learned it by getting on the bike, falling down a few times—until you suddenly got the hang of it, and now it became automatic.

Likewise, when you start speaking, there will come a point where it does not become automatic—it actually becomes *creative* because now the higher being that you are, the infinitely creative Being that you are, will begin to express itself through you. You will say things that you are surprised to hear from yourself because you had not thought of them before they were said. Had you not opened your mouth, would those ideas have come into your head? Nay, they would not, my beloved, for this is the essence of service—that you seek to help others by giving. In so giving, you receive.

The inexhaustible force of love

You have grown up in a world that is infused with the consciousness of death, which as one of its shadings has the entire illusion of lack, saying there is not enough. You have begun to realize that this is not true, although many of you still struggle to truly internalize what that means.

Let me at least give you an image that might help you. We have talked about the River of Life. Envision the River of Life as an inexhaustible, infinite ocean with all of the potential, all of the force, that is pent up in that water. The water is currently held back by a dam. Below the dam is a valley that is dry like a desert with only a few plants growing. All that water behind the dam could water that valley and make it fertile and green, but there are no openings in the dam through which the water can pass. Now imagine that someone gets up and starts drilling a hole through the dam. Imagine what will happen. Is there any doubt whatsoever that when that hole is made, the water will stream through it with all of the force behind it, for the water is eager and anxious to fulfill its mission?

There is an inexhaustible force of love and truth that is seeking to raise humankind. Our truth, our love, is being held back by the barriers created through people's free will. We can only express it when someone uses their free will to drill a hole and open themselves up for the light and the love and the wisdom and the truth to flow through them.

When you dare to make yourself an open door, certainly the Light will not leave you empty, will not leave you comfortless— as long as you remain in that emptiness of true service and do not fall into the temptation of seeking to control the Light by forming images of how the world should be saved. When you are willing to center in the heart and let your Higher Self or your ascended brothers and sisters speak through you, you will be amazed at what will come forth.

Certainly you do not need to say: "This is my Higher Self that has a message for you." Or: "El Morya told me to tell you this." Or: "Serapis Bey told me that you need discipline." These are images you project upon us. Be willing to recognize that you are an extension of a greater Being that has the solution to any problem, that can inspire any person by challenging their beliefs, their limitations, and giving them the hope of something higher. Then you will see that it will begin to flow through you. The eternal promise is: "You have been faithful over a few things, I will make thee ruler over many."

I, Jesus, say to you – and you can decide whether you feel included in this or not, but if you do not feel included, I suggest you look at why you do not feel included – and thus, I say to you: "Well done thou good and faithful servant." With that, I seal you in my joyous peace.

13 | I INVOKE
UNCONDITIONAL PEACE

In the name I AM THAT I AM, Jesus Christ, I call to my I AM Presence to flow through the I Will Be Presence that I AM and give this invocation with full power. I call to beloved Elohim Peace and Aloha, Archangel Uriel and Aurora, Nada and Jesus to help me overcome all blocks to my ability to communicate from complete peace. Help me be free from all patterns or forces within or without that oppose my communication from the heart and my oneness with my I AM Presence, including ...

[Make personal calls]

1. I acknowledge my Christ potential

1. I am one with the ascended master Jesus, and I am an expression of the God Flame of unconditional, infinite, never-ending, inexhaustible Joy.

> O Elohim Peace, in Unity's Flame,
> there is no more room for duality's game,
> we know that all form is from the same source,
> empowering us to plot a new course.

> **O Elohim Peace, the bell now you ring,**
> **causing all atoms to vibrate and sing,**
> **I now see that there is no separate thing,**
> **to my ego-based self I no longer cling.**

2. I consciously acknowledge that I am prepared at inner levels to accept the joyful message of the coming of Christ in my own being.

> O Elohim Peace, you help me to know,
> that Jesus has come your Flame to bestow,
> upon all who are ready to give up the strife,
> by following Christ into infinite life.

> **O Elohim Peace, through your eyes I see,**
> **that only in oneness will I ever be free,**
> **I give up the sense of a separate me,**
> **I AM crossing Samsara's turbulent sea.**

3. I am above the death consciousness, and I acknowledge that it is possible for me to embody the Christ consciousness on earth. I dare to embody Christhood and I dare to express it, I dare to communicate it to the world.

> O Elohim Peace, you show me the way,
> for clearing my mind from duality's fray,
> you pierce the illusions of both time and space,
> separation consumed by your Infinite Grace.

> **O Elohim Peace, what beauty your name,**
> **consuming within me duality's shame,**
> **It was through the vibration of your Golden Flame,**
> **that Christ the illusion of death overcame.**

4. I will show people that they have hope. They have hope that there is a better life and that they can attain it, if they are willing to look for it. I will bring that hope by demonstrating that there is a higher state of consciousness.

> O Elohim Peace, you bring now to earth,
> the unstoppable flame of Cosmic Rebirth,
> I give up the sense that something is mine,
> allowing your Light through my being to shine.

> **O Elohim Peace, through your tranquility,**
> **we are free from the chaos of duality,**
> **in oneness with God a new identity,**
> **we are raising the earth into Infinity.**

5. In oneness with Jesus, I stand in front of the high and the mighty of this world, the power elite of this world. I give witness to my spiritual knowledge, my spiritual being, my God realization.

> O Elohim Peace, in Unity's Flame,
> there is no more room for duality's game,
> we know that all form is from the same source,
> empowering us to plot a new course.

> **O Elohim Peace, the bell now you ring,**
> **causing all atoms to vibrate and sing,**
> **I now see that there is no separate thing,**
> **to my ego-based self I no longer cling.**

6. For me, God is not a theoretical concept that one can argue for or against endlessly. I have the final answer in experiencing the Living God within me.

> O Elohim Peace, you help me to know,
> that Jesus has come your Flame to bestow,
> upon all who are ready to give up the strife,
> by following Christ into infinite life.

> **O Elohim Peace, through your eyes I see,**
> **that only in oneness will I ever be free,**
> **I give up the sense of a separate me,**
> **I AM crossing Samsara's turbulent sea.**

7. In oneness with Jesus, I say: "I and my Father are One." This is my statement of joy. It is the proof that there is a God, the only proof that can ever be, given free will.

O Elohim Peace, you show me the way,
for clearing my mind from duality's fray,
you pierce the illusions of both time and space,
separation consumed by your Infinite Grace.

O Elohim Peace, what beauty your name,
consuming within me duality's shame,
It was through the vibration of your Golden Flame,
that Christ the illusion of death overcame.

8. In oneness with Jesus, I challenge the illusion that Jesus was the only son of God or the only one to ever attain personal Christhood. I too am the Living Christ in embodiment.

O Elohim Peace, you bring now to earth,
the unstoppable flame of Cosmic Rebirth,
I give up the sense that something is mine,
allowing your Light through my being to shine.

O Elohim Peace, through your tranquility,
we are free from the chaos of duality,
in oneness with God a new identity,
we are raising the earth into Infinity.

9. In oneness with Jesus, I challenge the illusions of the false teachers. I dare to speak and demonstrate that there is a reality beyond the duality consciousness. Each and every person can know that reality by finding Christ within.

Accelerate into Unity, I AM real,
Accelerate into Unity, all life heal,
Accelerate into Unity, I AM MORE,
Accelerate into Unity, all will soar.

Accelerate into Unity! (3X)
Beloved Peace and Aloha.
Accelerate into Unity! (3X)
Beloved Uriel and Aurora.
Accelerate into Unity! (3X)
Beloved Jesus and Nada.
Accelerate into Unity! (3X)
Beloved I AM.

2. I am willing to see Christ reality

1. In oneness with Jesus, I am the open door for challenging the catch-22 that causes people to look at every aspect of life through the filter of dualistic illusions. I dare to demonstrate my oneness with the Spirit of Truth, which cannot be fit into any database based on duality.

> Uriel Archangel, immense is the power,
> of angels of peace, all war to devour.
> The demons of war, no match for your light,
> consuming them all, with radiance so bright.

> **Uriel Archangel, use your great sword,**
> **Uriel Archangel, consume all discord,**
> **Uriel Archangel, we're of one accord,**
> **Uriel Archangel, we walk with the Lord.**

2. I accept that I am an individualization of the Creator's Being. The Creator is omnipresent, but my sense of self is focused at a localized point. The Creator sees everything from the omnipresent perspective; I see the world from my localized perspective.

> Uriel Archangel, intense is the sound,
> when millions of angels, their voices compound.
> They build a crescendo, piercing the night,
> life's glorious oneness revealed to our sight.

> **Uriel Archangel, use your great sword,**
> **Uriel Archangel, consume all discord,**
> **Uriel Archangel, we're of one accord,**
> **Uriel Archangel, we walk with the Lord.**

3. I recognize that the key to having an objective experience is to let the Christ in me help me see beyond my personal database. I am willing to experience the Presence of God and see beyond my present filter to experience a higher knowing.

Uriel Archangel, from out the Great Throne,
your millions of trumpets, sound the One Tone.
Consuming all discord with your harmony,
the sound of all sounds will set all life free.

Uriel Archangel, use your great sword,
Uriel Archangel, consume all discord,
Uriel Archangel, we're of one accord,
Uriel Archangel, we walk with the Lord.

4. I am willing to go through a conscious effort of questioning and challenging the assumptions and beliefs in my database. I am willing to see the world from a localized perspective that is free from dualistic beliefs.

Uriel Archangel, all war is now gone,
for you bring a message, from heart of the One.
The hearts of all men, now singing in peace,
the spirals of love, forever increase.

Uriel Archangel, use your great sword,
Uriel Archangel, consume all discord,
Uriel Archangel, we're of one accord,
Uriel Archangel, we walk with the Lord.

5. I am willing to see Christ reality, to see myself as a spiritual being, an extension of the Creator's Infinite Being, focused in a particular point in the finite world, but with an infinite potential to go beyond it and embrace infinity.

> Uriel Archangel, immense is the power,
> of angels of peace, all war to devour.
> The demons of war, no match for your light,
> consuming them all, with radiance so bright.

> **Uriel Archangel, use your great sword,**
> **Uriel Archangel, consume all discord,**
> **Uriel Archangel, we're of one accord,**
> **Uriel Archangel, we walk with the Lord.**

6. I am an open door for helping people see that there is something beyond the material world, and thus there is hope of escaping mortality, of escaping the consciousness of death. There is hope of escaping the fear that controls most people today.

> Uriel Archangel, intense is the sound,
> when millions of angels, their voices compound.
> They build a crescendo, piercing the night,
> life's glorious oneness revealed to our sight.

> **Uriel Archangel, use your great sword,**
> **Uriel Archangel, consume all discord,**
> **Uriel Archangel, we're of one accord,**
> **Uriel Archangel, we walk with the Lord.**

7. In oneness with Jesus, I say: "Oh death, where is thy victory?" For me, death has lost its sting. I am willing to go through the transformation of coming from death into life, from the death consciousness into the life consciousness. I am willing to speak that message from the heart.

Uriel Archangel, from out the Great Throne,
your millions of trumpets, sound the One Tone.
Consuming all discord with your harmony,
the sound of all sounds will set all life free.

Uriel Archangel, use your great sword,
Uriel Archangel, consume all discord,
Uriel Archangel, we're of one accord,
Uriel Archangel, we walk with the Lord.

8. I am willing to demonstrate that there is something beyond the death consciousness. I am willing to preach to those who are ready to go beyond fear and find an approach to spirituality that is not based on fear.

Uriel Archangel, all war is now gone,
for you bring a message, from heart of the One.
The hearts of all men, now singing in peace,
the spirals of love, forever increase.

Uriel Archangel, use your great sword,
Uriel Archangel, consume all discord,
Uriel Archangel, we're of one accord,
Uriel Archangel, we walk with the Lord.

9. In oneness with Jesus, I speak from the heart, I speak without fear. By knowing the heart of Jesus, I have attained non-attachment to other people's reactions.

> With angels I soar,
> as I reach for MORE.
> The angels so real,
> their love all will heal.
> The angels bring peace,
> all conflicts will cease.
> With angels of light,
> we soar to new height.

> **The rustling sound of angel wings,**
> **what joy as even matter sings,**
> **what joy as every atom rings,**
> **in harmony with angel wings.**

3. I will continually speak from the heart

1. I recognize that I cannot give true service to life unless I am fully at peace. I am willing to be centered in the heart, so that I can speak from the heart and shock people out of their present state of consciousness. I am willing to demonstrate that there is real hope of rising above the death consciousness.

> O Elohim Peace, in Unity's Flame,
> there is no more room for duality's game,
> we know that all form is from the same source,
> empowering us to plot a new course.

> **O Elohim Peace, the bell now you ring,**
> **causing all atoms to vibrate and sing,**
> **I now see that there is no separate thing,**
> **to my ego-based self I no longer cling.**

2. I am willing to show people unconditional love by turning the other cheek. I am willing to demonstrate that there is a higher way to respond than by responding to negativity with negativity.

> O Elohim Peace, you help me to know,
> that Jesus has come your Flame to bestow,
> upon all who are ready to give up the strife,
> by following Christ into infinite life.

> **O Elohim Peace, through your eyes I see,**
> **that only in oneness will I ever be free,**
> **I give up the sense of a separate me,**
> **I AM crossing Samsara's turbulent sea.**

3. I am the open door for demonstrating that there is some-thing beyond the dualistic struggle. I will speak from the heart and shock them into thinking about the possibility that there is something beyond their present state of consciousness.

O Elohim Peace, you show me the way,
for clearing my mind from duality's fray,
you pierce the illusions of both time and space,
separation consumed by your Infinite Grace.

O Elohim Peace, what beauty your name,
consuming within me duality's shame,
It was through the vibration of your Golden Flame,
that Christ the illusion of death overcame.

4. I will continually speak from the heart. I will be non-attached to the people who cannot be touched. I am willing to bring about the judgment of these souls by letting them rail against me and persecute me for Christ's sake.

O Elohim Peace, you bring now to earth,
the unstoppable flame of Cosmic Rebirth,
I give up the sense that something is mine,
allowing your Light through my being to shine.

O Elohim Peace, through your tranquility,
we are free from the chaos of duality,
in oneness with God a new identity,
we are raising the earth into Infinity.

5. I see that in order to continue to speak from the heart, I must be at peace. I can be at peace only when I am non-attached to other people's reactions. I will demonstrate non-attachment by speaking out in front of the high and the mighty, letting them do whatever they wish.

> O Elohim Peace, in Unity's Flame,
> there is no more room for duality's game,
> we know that all form is from the same source,
> empowering us to plot a new course.

> **O Elohim Peace, the bell now you ring,**
> **causing all atoms to vibrate and sing,**
> **I now see that there is no separate thing,**
> **to my ego-based self I no longer cling.**

6. I will demonstrate non-attachment by saying: "Father forgive them, for they know not what they do." I know that whatever people to do me, I will simply be non-attached and ask God to forgive them.

> O Elohim Peace, you help me to know,
> that Jesus has come your Flame to bestow,
> upon all who are ready to give up the strife,
> by following Christ into infinite life.

> **O Elohim Peace, through your eyes I see,**
> **that only in oneness will I ever be free,**
> **I give up the sense of a separate me,**
> **I AM crossing Samsara's turbulent sea.**

7. I know that whatever people do or say, I will give up any ghost represented by their consciousness and rise above it. I will not allow them to prevent my self-transcendence into ever higher levels of Christ consciousness.

O Elohim Peace, you show me the way,
for clearing my mind from duality's fray,
you pierce the illusions of both time and space,
separation consumed by your Infinite Grace.

O Elohim Peace, what beauty your name,
consuming within me duality's shame,
It was through the vibration of your Golden Flame,
that Christ the illusion of death overcame.

8. I see that Jesus spoke in many different ways, both gently and with authority. I will not limit my I AM presence and its ability to speak through me.

O Elohim Peace, you bring now to earth,
the unstoppable flame of Cosmic Rebirth,
I give up the sense that something is mine,
allowing your Light through my being to shine.

O Elohim Peace, through your tranquility,
we are free from the chaos of duality,
in oneness with God a new identity,
we are raising the earth into Infinity.

9. I am willing to let my I AM Presence speak through me in any way the situation warrants. I do not analyze with the outer mind, I surrender. I empty myself, and I let the Spirit fill me. I will take no thought for what I shall say, allowing the Spirit to speak through me.

> Accelerate into Unity, I AM real,
> Accelerate into Unity, all life heal,
> Accelerate into Unity, I AM MORE,
> Accelerate into Unity, all will soar.
>
> Accelerate into Unity! (3X)
> Beloved Peace and Aloha.
> Accelerate into Unity! (3X)
> Beloved Uriel and Aurora.
> Accelerate into Unity! (3X)
> Beloved Jesus and Nada.
> Accelerate into Unity! (3X)
> Beloved I AM.

4. I will start where I am

1. I am willing to work towards the point where the Spirit will always speak through me. I am willing to speak out, even if I am wrong or not at the highest vibration. I am willing to try and then learn from everything I do.

Master Nada, beauty's power,
unfolding like a sacred flower.
Master Nada, so sublime,
a will that conquers even time.

**O Holy Spirit, flow through me,
I am the open door for thee.
O mighty rushing stream of Light,
transcendence is my sacred right.**

2. I am willing to practice even though I am not perfect. I am willing to speak out based on the understanding and the attainment I have today. I am multiplying my talents and rising to a higher level of consciousness where I can receive *more* from the Spirit.

Master Nada, you bestow,
upon me wisdom's rushing flow.
Master Nada, mind so strong
rising on your wings of song.

**O Holy Spirit, flow through me,
I am the open door for thee.
O mighty rushing stream of Light,
transcendence is my sacred right.**

3. I hereby say to Jesus and my I AM Presence: "I am willing to multiply what you have given me thus far. I am willing to speak out based on my understanding, and I will continue to speak out."

Master Nada, precious scent,
your love is truly heaven-sent.
Master Nada, kind and soft
on wings of love we rise aloft.

O Holy Spirit, flow through me,
I am the open door for thee.
O mighty rushing stream of Light,
transcendence is my sacred right.

4. I consciously acknowledge that I have a right to speak out at my present level of awareness and understanding—and then learn from that, because that is the way to progress faster on the path.

Master Nada, mother light,
my heart is rising like a kite.
Master Nada, from your view,
all life is pure as morning dew.

O Holy Spirit, flow through me,
I am the open door for thee.
O mighty rushing stream of Light,
transcendence is my sacred right.

5. I am willing to leave my nets and follow Jesus. I am willing to express my present level of Christhood, for I know that the only mistake I could make is to refuse to experiment until I am perfect. Thus, I will follow Christ from my present state and then transcend that state.

Master Nada, truth you bring,
as morning birds in love do sing.
Master Nada, I now feel,
your love that all four bodies heal.

O Holy Spirit, flow through me,
I am the open door for thee.
O mighty rushing stream of Light,
transcendence is my sacred right.

6. I will let Jesus take me towards the point where the higher being that I AM, the infinitely creative Being that I AM, will begin to express itself through me. I realize that the essence of service is to help others by giving. And in so giving, I receive.

Master Nada, serve in peace,
as all emotions I release.
Master Nada, life is fun,
my solar plexus is a sun.

O Holy Spirit, flow through me,
I am the open door for thee.
O mighty rushing stream of Light,
transcendence is my sacred right.

7. I am willing to be an open door for the inexhaustible force of love and truth that is seeking to raise humankind. I am using my free will to open myself up for the light and the love and the wisdom and the truth to flow through me.

Master Nada, love is free,
with no conditions binding me.
Master Nada, rise above,
all human forms of lesser love.

**O Holy Spirit, flow through me,
I am the open door for thee.
O mighty rushing stream of Light,
transcendence is my sacred right.**

8. I dare to make myself an open door, and the Light will not leave me empty, will not leave me comfortless. I will remain in the emptiness of true service. I will center in the heart and let my I AM Presence and ascended brothers and sisters speak through me.

Master Nada, balance all,
the seven rays upon my call.
Master Nada, rise and shine,
your radiant beauty most divine.

**O Holy Spirit, flow through me,
I am the open door for thee.
O mighty rushing stream of Light,
transcendence is my sacred right.**

9. I recognize that I am an extension of a greater Being that has the solution to any problem. I accept that my I AM Presence can inspire any person by challenging their beliefs, their limitations, and giving them the hope of something higher. I accept the eternal promise: "You have been faithful over a few things, I will make thee ruler over many things."

> Nada Dear, your Presence here,
> filling up my inner sphere.
> Life is now a sacred flow,
> God Peace I do on all bestow.

> **O Holy Spirit, flow through me,**
> **I am the open door for thee.**
> **O mighty rushing stream of Light,**
> **transcendence is my sacred right.**

Sealing:

In the name of the Divine Mother, I fully accept that the power of these calls is used to set free the Ma-ter light, so it can outpicture the perfect vision of Christ for my own life, for all people and for the planet. In the name I AM THAT I AM, it is done! Amen.

14 | OVERCOME YOUR DRAMAS

A dictation by Saint Germain, representing the Seventh Ray of freedom.

S aint Germain I AM, and I AM free! Why are you not free? Because you are not me!

What is the key to being free? You should know by now that everything is an expression of the Creator's Being that has taken on a certain characteristic, be it love, wisdom, power, truth, peace or freedom. You too are out of the Creator's Being.

What is the key to experiencing, and being the open door for, the expression of a particular quality, such as freedom? It is to allow your own being, your conscious self − or however you wish to see it − to become one with the flame of that God quality, as I AM one with the God quality of freedom. You will then be the open door for that God quality to be expressed to the earth, to be expressed in the earth, to be expressed on the surface of the earth, and to be expressed in the hearts of men and women, as they are willing to *be* freedom.

Your drama takes away your freedom

What then is the key to being free? It is, of course, to realize the reality that what prevents you from being free is that you have created a drama, a personal story, that you think you have to keep outplaying indefinitely. You somehow have become trapped in it, identified with it. You think that the drama gives you something that you need, something you cannot live without.

That something is – as has been expressed by other masters – something from the material world that you think you need, that you think will complete you. As has been said before – and as we will say again until you finally get it – you can never be fulfilled by anything in the material world. You can only be fulfilled by something from the spiritual realm, namely one of the flames of God. You can only experience something from the spiritual realm by being the open door for it to stream forth in the material realm and thus raise up all life.

You know that I was embodied as the person who gave birth to a substantial portion of the Shakespearian plays, thus you should realize that I enjoy drama as much as anyone. Even when you watch other people outplay a drama, you are out-picturing certain roles in your own mind, depending on how you see the drama, how you look at it, how you look at the persons who are on the forefront of it. Your way of looking at the drama, your way of experiencing it, will – if you are honest and willing – show you your own drama.

Are you embarrassed by certain things? Then you are out-playing a certain drama. Are you afraid that certain things will be said? Then *that* is your drama, giving you the fear, the desire to limit what can be said in a conversation. When you have a drama that gives you a need to limit what can be said, then you obviously are not free to let communication flow from the heart, for you seek to restrict that flow.

Free communication has no standard

Sometimes you may think that communication from the heart has to live up to a certain standard for what you believe is "heartfelt," or "spiritual" or "loving" communication. As has been explained earlier, sometimes the heart can take on a certain coloring, depending on the person's basic world view. If the person is still willing to speak in the open, then they have an opportunity – by bringing it out in the open in front of other people – to see it in a different light than they have seen it before. Therefore, they move closer to that breakthrough point where they finally clearly see it for what it is. They see that it is only something their conscious selves have taken on, that they are so much more. They can finally make that decision: "I no longer need this drama in order to get what I need, for I know I can get it from inside myself."

Your personal drama is like a maze. You are trapped in the maze and you cannot find your way out. You have come to believe – because you have come to identify yourself with the drama – that you are trapped there by external forces or other people and that you cannot escape. You will never escape the drama – the maze, the labyrinth – until you realize that the drama was not created by God, by other people, by fate, by chance. It was created by *you!*

You are the only one who can find your way out of the maze, for you are the only one who can decide that you will no longer see yourself as the person who is trapped in the maze. You will shift your focus and realize that you are more than that person, more than the maze, more than the subconscious database that prevents you from getting out.

Be open to the Holy Spirit

What does this have to do with communication from the heart? We have talked about how you can rise on the spiritual path through the initiations of the different rays. Jesus talked about how you come to a point of desiring only to serve the All, being at peace in recognizing that you are part of the All and that you are not threatened by any person whatsoever, no matter their response.

Now take this to the next level of the initiations of the Seventh Ray of Freedom where those who pass the initiations on the Seventh Ray can truly become mouthpieces for the flow of the Holy Spirit to express itself through them. The Spirit can give a certain person exactly what that person needs at that particular moment in order to receive the best possible opportunity to see at least part of his or her own drama. They can have an opportunity to know that there is *more* and to choose to espouse it.

You cannot know this with the outer mind, no matter how well you know a person, no matter how well you know human psychology. You cannot intellectually know what a person needs at any given moment. The more you study a person, the more you think you know them – the more you study psychology, the more you think you know psychology – what you are really doing is reinforcing your subconscious database. In any given situation, you are seeking to make the person fit into your database. You respond based on the preprogrammed responses that have entered your database in the past.

In some cases you will be right and you will give the persons what they need. You cannot always be right this way, especially when you are dealing with people that you do not know at all, or do not know as well as you think you know them. The more you think you know a person, the less you actually know them—at least, if your knowledge of them is based on the database of their past actions and choices.

A subtle form of black magic

Although there may be a certain probability that a person will make the same choice today that he has made a hundred times in the past, the Law of Free Will makes it clear that there is no certainty that a person will keep repeating the same choices. This is the lesson that science and humankind at large should have learned from the findings of quantum physics where nothing can be predicted with certainty until the experiment is made. If you hold in your mind the image: "Oh, this person is such-and-such, and this person will outplay this drama and will do such-and-such," then you are superimposing that image upon the person and actually making it more difficult for the person to make a different choice.

This is – to be brutally honest with you – a form of black magic where you do not acknowledge the reality that any lifestream, no matter how trapped they have been in a certain pattern, has the potential to make a different choice at any moment. Holding the immaculate concept means that you do not hold the image that a person will do what they have "always done," but you hold the image that a person will at any moment make the highest possible choice they can make in that situation.

Your communication will be completely adapted to helping that person make that choice. You will not judge what should be said or what should not be said—you will let the Holy Spirit blow where it listeth, flow through you and say something that you had not even thought about, that you would not have thought about in a million years, as they say. You are as surprised as the other person at what comes out.

This is what happens to those who have risen up through the seven rays and who come to the Seventh Ray with peace from Jesus and therefore can truly espouse the freedom of Saint Germain, the Freedom Flame that I AM. They can allow the Holy Spirit to blow where it listeth, instead of seeking to force it into a certain pattern or matrix that they think will make them safe.

Have you passed the initiations of the seven rays?

What happens to those who have not passed these initiations? There are indeed many who think they have risen to some level where they are qualified to tell other people what to do, how to live their lives, how to live their path and how to overcome this or that problem. I am not saying that you are not qualified, I am not saying that you have to be perfect before you can speak out. You should, as has been said, speak out at any level. What I am endeavoring to show you here is that you have, if you are willing, a sense of co-measurement of whether you have actually passed the initiations of the seven rays.

The fact of the matter is this: If you speak out and you do not get the response that you expected, then you have not fully passed the initiations of the seven rays and cannot fully speak from the heart. If you get a response that causes you to go into any negative state of mind, then that shows that you have an attachment to the outcome. You are not free; you are not speaking freely to another.

I am not saying that if this is your experience, then you should now stop speaking out. As has been said, if you are not willing to practice and multiply the talents, you will never rise higher. I am simply giving you a sense of co-measurement that attachment to an outcome is not freedom—it cannot be freedom.

What you can do in order to accelerate your own growth is that you can look at yourself, and you can see what kind of reaction you typically have when you speak out to other people and they respond in a way that causes you to react to their response. How do you react? Then trace that back—what is the feeling? Get in touch with the feeling. Then see beyond the feeling—what is the thought behind the feeling? Analyze, categorize, intuit about the thought and what it actually says about your view of yourself, other people and life.

Then go beyond the thought and get in touch with what is the underlying pattern, the basic assumption that forms the foundation for your database. Consider what that says about your sense of identity and how you see yourself, how you see yourself in relation to the world and how you see yourself in relation to God. Notice whether you see yourself relating to the external God or you are beginning to be more in tune with the internal God. This is an essential key to your freedom.

A cost-benefit analysis of pain

Every master who has ascended from earth has done precisely this: self-observation—objective, non-emotional, non-judgmental, non-blaming, self-revelation. This means being willing to have that revelation of what is pure and impure, what is not quite there, what keeps you trapped in certain reactionary patterns. Every ascended master has done this until the moment they ascended. Every person who has reached spiritual maturity is doing this constantly. Those who are not doing this constantly are those who are so trapped in their dramas that they are not able to do this. They think that if they see something in themselves that is not according to a certain standard, then it will cause them pain or self-condemnation.

What do you do if you honestly realize that this is the case for you—that you are still so wounded that you find it difficult to look at yourself without going into fear or self-condemnation? What do you do, my beloved? There is not necessarily only one answer, but the more intense the pain, the more you might consider that there can come a point where you simply have to make a very hard, objective calculation—kind of a cost-benefit analysis, as they say in the business world. You may have to say to yourself: "Do I want to live the rest of this embodiment experiencing the pain and discomfort I am experiencing right now?" If the answer is "Yes," then by all means pursue that, for you have the total freedom of the Law of Free Will to do this. I have no judgment whatsoever of you. I simply state that then I, as the God of Freedom, cannot help you.

If you come to the conclusion that you do not want to live the rest of your life in this pain, then you need to realize that the pain comes from a wound. Looking at the wound will cause you more intense pain than you have right now. The fact is that the personal drama that you are outplaying has allowed you to cope with the pain to a certain degree where it has become familiar, tolerable, perhaps even giving you a sense of contentment that this is just the way life has to be. You can deal with the daily pain in many cases, even though it is there constantly.

Looking at the wound and the mechanism behind it will cause you a more intense pain. Nevertheless, if you work through the wound and heal it, then not only will the intense pain disappear but the constant numbing pain will also disappear. It is, my beloved, absolutely the only way that anyone has ever found any healing whatsoever.

There is no shortcut

As an ascended being I can assure you there is no shortcut! You will not enter the kingdom of God without looking at the beam in your own eye. Christ said it 2,000 years ago. It is a timeless, eternal truth, also expressed by the Buddha. It will not change because the Law of Free Will will not change. What you have created for yourself, as a self-image that keeps you trapped in a painful state, can only be changed by your own choices.

It is almost like some of the choices that doctors can face, for example in a war, where a wounded soldier is brought in and they have the choice that either they cut off a leg or the person will die. What do you do in that situation? You have to do what is best for the person's survival. Likewise, for yourself: Will you keep living with the pain that you have, or will you go in and do whatever is necessary—including seeking professional help in the psychological field, which many people who have made progress on the path have done. Will you do that, and then take a giant leap forward?

I can assure you that no matter what your pain might tell you, there is no wound that cannot be healed. It is absolutely impossible to enter any kind of prison from which you cannot escape. You can always be free. The fact of the matter is that your freedom from any condition is just a few choices away. If you could make one choice, you could instantly escape from your present condition. You can go through the extreme process of finally giving up defending your drama and being willing to go through the sense of spiritual death. If you go through the process of not knowing who you are, and then realizing that you are not the human, you are not the wounds, you are not the drama, you will open yourself up to that direct inner experience that you are *more*.

The choice, then, is yours. You are not a victim of anyone or anything but your own past choices. Any past choice can be transcended by making a better choice in the present, not in the future, my beloved, for the future never arrives. The moment to make choices is always now. The question is which "now" in the string of "nows" in your life you will make the now where you finally make that decision to do something about the wounds and the pain, rather than trying to live with them and actually defend your pain, defend your drama.

Helping others escape the drama

This brings us back to communication. Imagine the doctor faced with a wounded soldier. He has absolutely no desire whatsoever to cut off the person's leg, or to do some other procedure that causes pain, but nevertheless he is there to save the person's life if at all possible. Imagine that you are meeting a person or that you are dealing with a person – and many of you do not even have to imagine it, for you are dealing with such persons on a daily basis – who is totally trapped in their drama, in great pain, perhaps even suicidal or in other ways schizophrenic or out of balance. You are faced with a similar choice. What do you do to help the person escape the trap of their personal drama?

When a person is identified with their drama and is acting out the drama that person is constantly seeking to pull all other people into their drama. The drama does not only involve that person. The person has created a drama that might contain the entire world, and the person has then assigned – as a scriptwriter assigns roles – various roles to all the people that it encounters, including you. The person simply wants to get all people to live up to their predefined roles so that they reaffirm the reality of the drama. Why is the person caught in a drama? As we have said, because you assign ultimate reality to the dualistic beliefs in your database. If you really want to help that person be free, you cannot play the role they want you to play. That only reaffirms their prison, their sense of being trapped in the drama, the sense of the reality of the drama. You must refuse to play that role.

What will happen to the person, what will they feel when you refuse to play the role? They might feel angry, they might feel hurt, they might feel afraid. My point is that when you refuse to play the role they have assigned to you, you will cause them more pain—you will intensify their pain, just like a doctor might have to cause physical pain in order to save a patient.

The question is, my beloved: "Are you willing to do this?" Are you willing to serve in that capacity? Can you actually be so free in yourself that you can refuse to enter another person's drama, and thereby let that drama be intensified in your presence until the person becomes so agitated that he or she finally comes to that breaking point of saying: "I can't do this anymore. I give up."

I wish I could give you a sense of co-measurement of the intensity of love that we of the ascended masters have for you— all of you, all human beings. Especially, my beloved, those who are on the spiritual path, and who therefore have risen to a level where they have the potential to manifest Christhood in this embodiment—but there is one last drama that they have not let go of.

These are the students where we might use rather extreme measures to expose their dramas. How do we feel when we have a student that we know is committed at inner levels to manifesting Christhood, but there is that last element of ego. How can we let them go, still defending the drama, the illusion? We desire to do whatever is possible to help that person see beyond the drama.

In many cases we cannot reach them because they are not hearing us. That is why we need you because you can "be in their face," so to speak. You can confront them physically so they cannot ignore you, they cannot shut you out. Are you willing to serve in that capacity? If you are, then you are truly free. This is freedom where you can serve as the ultimate teacher who will not affirm another person's illusions, but will keep challenging those illusions in various ways, simply refusing to step into the drama. At the same time refusing to go away so that the person can forget and ignore them.

When to leave others alone

Is it not always easy, my beloved, to find an excuse and say: "Oh, that person isn't open, she is not willing to change?" Sometimes it is valid to leave a person alone. Many of you are facing people in your family that you have had conflicts with throughout this lifetime, and actually for many lifetimes, if you will hear it. In some cases you can come to a point where you have worked on resolving in yourself the source of that conflict. When you have resolved it in yourself and the other person is still not willing to work on it – or even consider that they have anything to work on – then it can be perfectly valid for you to say: "I will move on for a time."

This does not mean that you say you permanently leave another person behind and will not speak to them. Should they ever come back to you and desire to resolve it, then you will be there for them. It does mean that you say: "You have had enough of my attention, and I must move on to someone else that I can actually help, for they are willing to change themselves."

You must also be open to the potential that there can be some people who fit the criteria I just described, namely that they have the potential to manifest Christhood in this lifetime and there is that one last illusion that they have not seen. They might need a very severe exposure to "extreme reality therapy," as we might call it, in order to finally see it—see it for what it is. Then they actually have the real choice that they have not been willing to give themselves, for they have been so trapped in defending the illusion.

Sometimes in the beginning – before you have attained complete freedom – this can be painful to you. Some people have been used to say things to people, or even say things to the general community, that they really did not want to say because they knew the reaction. They were willing to say it, and as such grew immensely from the experience. Of course, you also grow in your ability for us to use you and therefore might not have to be as direct and confrontational as when you are tested in non-attachment. You might learn from that and again consider in yourself whether you are reluctant or afraid to be direct, to be open, to be free in what you say to other people.

You are here to heal humankind

Let me go back to the doctor analogy and say that you are the doctors who have come to earth, and the patient that is sick is humankind. Are you willing to play that role—are you willing to be direct and open; to be free?

I am not asking you here to force yourselves to play a role that will cause you pain. I am asking you to resolve the pain so that you are not playing a role. You are freely expressing what you have freely received from Above. The Holy Spirit can blow where it listeth through you, and thus perform that psychological-spiritual surgery that another person needs.

I can assure you that when you come to that point of freedom, there is no pain, even when others are in pain. There is only joy and love. This is why you can serve to first challenge a person, and then – when they have started to see what they need to see – you can give them that unconditional love. You can do this even if in the process of coming to see it, they have been quite unpleasant with you, accusing you of this or that, crying, trying to pull you into the drama in any way—even trying to hurt you deliberately, as some will do as they lash out from their wounded selves.

When you are free to remain above the reaction, then you will not be touched by this. It will pass right through you. When the person comes to the point of having given up, then you can be there with the unconditional love and with the wisdom that the person is now open to. The person can process and therefore attain greater clarity, as they are willing and able. Or, if the person is so wounded that they simply cannot stand the sight of you for a while, you can be non-attached to that. Even if the person comes back ten years later, you will be there with unconditional love, for you have no wounds you need to act out towards the person before you are willing to talk to them again.

You see, my beloved, I AM free. I desire you to be free. I am not seeking to force you. In fact, it is your own drama that is the only force that forces you to do anything. I simply desire you to know that freedom is a real option and that freedom is a choice, and that that choice can be made by only one person, and who is that person? [Audience says, "Me!"] Exactly!

With that I thank you for your attention, for your presence, and I seal you in the unconditional love that is flowing freely through me as unconditional, infinite Freedom!

15 | I INVOKE
UNCONDITIONAL FREEDOM

In the name I AM THAT I AM, Jesus Christ, I call to my I AM Presence to flow through the I Will Be Presence that I AM and give this invocation with full power. I call to beloved Arcturus and Victoria, Archangel Zadkiel and Amethyst, Saint Germain and Portia to help me overcome all blocks to my ability to communicate from complete freedom. Help me be free from all patterns or forces within or without that oppose my communication from the heart and my oneness with my I AM Presence, including ...

[Make personal calls]

1. I am willing to transcend my drama

1. In oneness with Saint Germain, I allow my Conscious You to become one with the flame of the God quality of Freedom. I am the open door for that God quality to be expressed in the earth, and to be expressed in the hearts of men and women, as they are willing to be freedom.

> Beloved Arcturus, release now the flow,
> of Violet Flame to help all life grow,
> in ever-expanding circles of Light,
> it pulses within every atom so bright.

> **Beloved Arcturus, thou Elohim Free,**
> **I open my heart to your reality,**
> **expanding my heart into Infinity,**
> **your flame is the key to my God-victory.**

2. Beloved I AM Presence and Saint Germain, I want to be free. Help me see the drama, the personal story, that I think I have to keep outplaying indefinitely. Help me see that I do not have to remain trapped in this drama because it does not give me anything I need, anything I cannot live without.

> Beloved Arcturus, be with me alway,
> reborn, I am ready to face a new day,
> I have no attachments to life here on earth,
> I claim a new life in your Flame of Rebirth.

> **Beloved Arcturus, your Violet Flame pure,**
> **is for every ailment the ultimate cure,**
> **against it no darkness could ever endure,**
> **my freedom it will forever ensure.**

3. Beloved I AM Presence and Saint Germain, help me see I can never be fulfilled by anything in the material world. I can only be fulfilled by experiencing one of the flames of God. I can only experience this by being the open door for it to stream forth in the material realm and raise up all life.

Beloved Arcturus, your bright violet fire,
now fills every atom, raising them higher,
the space in each atom all filled with your light,
as matter itself is shining so bright.

Beloved Arcturus, your transforming Grace,
empowers me now every challenge to face,
as your violet light floods my inner space,
towards my ascension I willingly race.

4. Beloved I AM Presence and Saint Germain, I am willing to see my drama by looking at how I experience and react to life. Help me see how my drama gives me a need to limit what can be said. Help me be free to let communication flow from the heart, without letting my drama restrict that flow.

Beloved Arcturus, bring in a new age,
help earth and humanity turn a new page,
your transforming light gives me certainty,
Saint Germain's Golden Age is a reality.

Beloved Arcturus, I surrender all fear,
I AM feeling your Presence so tangibly near,
with your Freedom's Song filling my ear,
I know that to God I AM ever so dear.

5. Beloved I AM Presence and Saint Germain, help me experience the breakthrough where I see my drama for what it is. I see it is something my Conscious You has taken on and I make the decision: "I no longer need this drama in order to get what I need, for I know I can get it from inside myself."

Beloved Arcturus, release now the flow,
of Violet Flame to help all life grow,
in ever-expanding circles of Light,
it pulses within every atom so bright.

Beloved Arcturus, thou Elohim Free,
I open my heart to your reality,
expanding my heart into Infinity,
your flame is the key to my God-victory.

6. Beloved I AM Presence and Saint Germain, help me see that my personal drama is like a maze because I have come to identify myself with the drama. Help me realize that the drama was not created by God, by other people, by fate or by chance. It was created by *me!*

Beloved Arcturus, be with me alway,
reborn, I am ready to face a new day,
I have no attachments to life here on earth,
I claim a new life in your Flame of Rebirth.

Beloved Arcturus, your Violet Flame pure,
is for every ailment the ultimate cure,
against it no darkness could ever endure,
my freedom it will forever ensure.

7. Beloved I AM Presence and Saint Germain, help me see that I am the only one who can find my way out of the maze. I am the only one who can decide that I will shift my focus and realize that I am more than the person, more than the maze, more than the subconscious database that prevents me from getting out.

Beloved Arcturus, your bright violet fire,
now fills every atom, raising them higher,
the space in each atom all filled with your light,
as matter itself is shining so bright.

**Beloved Arcturus, your transforming Grace,
empowers me now every challenge to face,
as your violet light floods my inner space,
towards my ascension I willingly race.**

8. Beloved I AM Presence and Saint Germain, help me pass the initiations on the Seventh Ray and become a mouthpiece for the flow of the Holy Spirit to express itself through me. I will let the Spirit give people exactly what they need in order to receive the best possible opportunity to see their own dramas.

Beloved Arcturus, bring in a new age,
help earth and humanity turn a new page,
your transforming light gives me certainty,
Saint Germain's Golden Age is a reality.

**Beloved Arcturus, I surrender all fear,
I AM feeling your Presence so tangibly near,
with your Freedom's Song filling my ear,
I know that to God I AM ever so dear.**

9. Beloved I AM Presence and Saint Germain, I unconditionally surrender all images I hold of what other people should or will do based on the past. I will no longer superimpose any images upon others but set them free to outplay their free will independently of me or my drama.

Accelerate into Freedom, I AM real,
Accelerate into Freedom, all life heal,
Accelerate into Freedom, I AM MORE,
Accelerate into Freedom, all will soar.

Accelerate into Freedom! (3X)
Beloved Arcturus and Victoria.
Accelerate into Freedom! (3X)
Beloved Zadkiel and Amethyst.
Accelerate into Freedom! (3X)
Beloved Saint Germain.
Accelerate into Freedom! (3X)
Beloved I AM.

2. I am willing to have my wounds healed

1. Beloved I AM Presence and Saint Germain, help me overcome all tendency to use black magic against other people. I acknowledge that any lifestream has the potential to make a different choice at any moment. I hold the immaculate concept that a person will make the highest possible choice.

Zadkiel Archangel, your flow is so swift,
in your violet light, I instantly shift,
into a vibration in which I am free,
from all limitations of the lesser me.

Zadkiel Archangel, encircle the earth,
Zadkiel Archangel, with your violet girth,
Zadkiel Archangel, unstoppable mirth,
Zadkiel Archangel, our planet's rebirth.

2. I have risen up through the seven rays and I come to the
Seventh Ray with peace from Jesus. I truly espouse the Freedom
Flame of Saint Germain. I allow the Holy Spirit to blow where
it listeth, instead of seeking to force it into a certain pattern or
matrix that I think will make me safe.

Zadkiel Archangel, I truly aspire,
to being the master of your violet fire.
Wielding the power, of your alchemy,
I use Sacred Word, to set all life free.

Zadkiel Archangel, encircle the earth,
Zadkiel Archangel, with your violet girth,
Zadkiel Archangel, unstoppable mirth,
Zadkiel Archangel, our planet's rebirth.

3. Beloved I AM Presence and Saint Germain, give me a sense of co-measurement of whether I have passed the initiations of the seven rays. I am willing to look at my reactions when I speak. I recognize that when I go into any negative state of mind, it shows that I have an attachment to the outcome.

Zadkiel Archangel, your violet light,
transforming the earth, with unstoppable might.
So swiftly our planet, beginning to spin,
with legions of angels, our victory we win.

Zadkiel Archangel, encircle the earth,
Zadkiel Archangel, with your violet girth,
Zadkiel Archangel, unstoppable mirth,
Zadkiel Archangel, our planet's rebirth.

4. Beloved I AM Presence and Saint Germain, help me see what kind of reaction I typically have when I speak out and other people respond in a way that causes me to react. Help me trace back the feeling, get in touch with the feeling.

Zadkiel Archangel, your violet flame,
the earth and humanity, never the same.
Saint Germain's Golden Age, is a reality,
what glorious wonder, I joyously see.

Zadkiel Archangel, encircle the earth,
Zadkiel Archangel, with your violet girth,
Zadkiel Archangel, unstoppable mirth,
Zadkiel Archangel, our planet's rebirth.

5. Beloved I AM Presence and Saint Germain, help me see beyond the feeling to what is the thought behind the feeling. Help me analyze and intuit about the thought and what it says about my view of myself, other people and life.

Zadkiel Archangel, your flow is so swift,
in your violet light, I instantly shift,
into a vibration in which I am free,
from all limitations of the lesser me.

Zadkiel Archangel, encircle the earth,
Zadkiel Archangel, with your violet girth,
Zadkiel Archangel, unstoppable mirth,
Zadkiel Archangel, our planet's rebirth.

6. Beloved I AM Presence and Saint Germain, help me go beyond the thought and get in touch with the underlying pattern, the basic assumption that forms the foundation for my database. Help me see what that says about my sense of identity. Help me stop relating to the external God and tune in to the internal God.

Zadkiel Archangel, I truly aspire,
to being the master of your violet fire.
Wielding the power, of your alchemy,
I use Sacred Word, to set all life free.

Zadkiel Archangel, encircle the earth,
Zadkiel Archangel, with your violet girth,
Zadkiel Archangel, unstoppable mirth,
Zadkiel Archangel, our planet's rebirth.

7. Beloved I AM Presence and Saint Germain, help me go through the process of self-observation—objective, non-emotional, non-judgmental, non-blaming, self-revelation. I am willing to see what is pure and impure, what keeps me trapped in certain reactionary patterns.

Zadkiel Archangel, your violet light,
transforming the earth, with unstoppable might.
So swiftly our planet, beginning to spin,
with legions of angels, our victory we win.

Zadkiel Archangel, encircle the earth,
Zadkiel Archangel, with your violet girth,
Zadkiel Archangel, unstoppable mirth,
Zadkiel Archangel, our planet's rebirth.

8. Beloved I AM Presence and Saint Germain, help me make an objective calculation, a cost-benefit analysis. Truly, I do not want to live the rest of this embodiment experiencing the pain and discomfort I am experiencing right now. Help me see the wound that is causing my pain.

Zadkiel Archangel, your violet flame,
the earth and humanity, never the same.
Saint Germain's Golden Age, is a reality,
what glorious wonder, I joyously see.

Zadkiel Archangel, encircle the earth,
Zadkiel Archangel, with your violet girth,
Zadkiel Archangel, unstoppable mirth,
Zadkiel Archangel, our planet's rebirth.

9. Beloved I AM Presence and Saint Germain, help me look at my wound even if it causes me a temporary pain. Help me work through the wound and heal it. Help me see the choices that caused the wound and then I will consciously change those choices. I am willing to take a giant leap forward.

> With angels I soar,
> as I reach for MORE.
> The angels so real,
> their love all will heal.
> The angels bring peace,
> all conflicts will cease.
> With angels of light,
> we soar to new height.

> **The rustling sound of angel wings,**
> **what joy as even matter sings,**
> **what joy as every atom rings,**
> **in harmony with angel wings.**

3. I will help others transcend their dramas

1. Beloved I AM Presence and Saint Germain, help me experience that no matter what pain I feel, there is no wound that cannot be healed. Help me know that my freedom from any condition is just a few choices away. Help me see the one choice that could help me instantly escape from my present condition.

> Beloved Arcturus, release now the flow,
> of Violet Flame to help all life grow,
> in ever-expanding circles of Light,
> it pulses within every atom so bright.

> **Beloved Arcturus, thou Elohim Free,**
> **I open my heart to your reality,**
> **expanding my heart into Infinity,**
> **your flame is the key to my God-victory.**

2. Beloved I AM Presence and Saint Germain, help me give up defending my drama and go through the sense of spiritual death. I am willing to go through the process of not knowing who I am, and then realizing that I am not the human, I am not the wounds, I am not the drama. I am open to the direct experience that I am *more*.

> Beloved Arcturus, be with me alway,
> reborn, I am ready to face a new day,
> I have no attachments to life here on earth,
> I claim a new life in your Flame of Rebirth.

Beloved Arcturus, your Violet Flame pure,
is for every ailment the ultimate cure,
against it no darkness could ever endure,
my freedom it will forever ensure.

3. Beloved I AM Presence and Saint Germain, help me see that I am not a victim of anyone or anything but my own past choices. Any past choice can be transcended by making a better choice in the present, for the moment to make choices is always now. I am NOW willing to do something about the wounds and the pain, rather than trying to live with them and actually defend my pain, defend my drama.

Beloved Arcturus, your bright violet fire,
now fills every atom, raising them higher,
the space in each atom all filled with your light,
as matter itself is shining so bright.

Beloved Arcturus, your transforming Grace,
empowers me now every challenge to face,
as your violet light floods my inner space,
towards my ascension I willingly race.

4. Beloved I AM Presence and Saint Germain, help me be free of my dramas, so I can serve to help other people escape their dramas. Help me see when people are seeking to pull me into their dramas. Help me see that I cannot help others by being pulled into their dramas, by playing the role they want me to play.

Beloved Arcturus, bring in a new age,
help earth and humanity turn a new page,
your transforming light gives me certainty,
Saint Germain's Golden Age is a reality.

Beloved Arcturus, I surrender all fear,
I AM feeling your Presence so tangibly near,
with your Freedom's Song filling my ear,
I know that to God I AM ever so dear.

5. I recognize that when I refuse to play the role others have assigned to me, I will intensify their pain. I am willing to do this, I am willing to serve in that capacity. I am so free in myself that I refuse to enter other people's dramas, helping them come to the breaking point of saying: "I can't do this anymore. I give up."

Beloved Arcturus, release now the flow,
of Violet Flame to help all life grow,
in ever-expanding circles of Light,
it pulses within every atom so bright.

Beloved Arcturus, thou Elohim Free,
I open my heart to your reality,
expanding my heart into Infinity,
your flame is the key to my God-victory.

6. Saint Germain, give me a sense of co-measurement of the intensity of love that the ascended masters have for us, for all human beings. Help me feel the love you have for those who are on the spiritual path, those who have the potential to manifest Christhood, but there is one last drama they have not surrendered.

> Beloved Arcturus, be with me alway,
> reborn, I am ready to face a new day,
> I have no attachments to life here on earth,
> I claim a new life in your Flame of Rebirth.
>
> **Beloved Arcturus, your Violet Flame pure,**
> **is for every ailment the ultimate cure,**
> **against it no darkness could ever endure,**
> **my freedom it will forever ensure.**

7. Saint Germain, help me tune in to your love and your desire to do whatever is possible to help a spiritual student see beyond the drama. I am willing to help you, to "be in their face," to confront them so they cannot ignore me, they cannot shut me out.

> Beloved Arcturus, your bright violet fire,
> now fills every atom, raising them higher,
> the space in each atom all filled with your light,
> as matter itself is shining so bright.
>
> **Beloved Arcturus, your transforming Grace,**
> **empowers me now every challenge to face,**
> **as your violet light floods my inner space,**
> **towards my ascension I willingly race.**

8. Saint Germain, help me have the freedom to serve as the ultimate teacher, who will not affirm another person's illusions, but will keep challenging those illusions, refusing to step into the drama. At the same time I refuse to go away so that the person cannot forget or ignore me.

Beloved Arcturus, bring in a new age,
help earth and humanity turn a new page,
your transforming light gives me certainty,
Saint Germain's Golden Age is a reality.

**Beloved Arcturus, I surrender all fear,
I AM feeling your Presence so tangibly near,
with your Freedom's Song filling my ear,
I know that to God I AM ever so dear.**

9. Saint Germain, help me have the discernment to know when it is valid to leave a person alone. Help me resolve in myself the source of conflict. Help me know when it is valid to say: "I will move on for a time. You have had enough of my attention, and I must move on to someone else that I can actually help, for they are willing to change themselves."

Accelerate into Freedom, I AM real,
Accelerate into Freedom, all life heal,
Accelerate into Freedom, I AM MORE,
Accelerate into Freedom, all will soar.

Accelerate into Freedom! (3X)
Beloved Arcturus and Victoria.
Accelerate into Freedom! (3X)
Beloved Zadkiel and Amethyst.
Accelerate into Freedom! (3X)
Beloved Saint Germain.
Accelerate into Freedom! (3X)
Beloved I AM.

4. I am the instrument of Saint Germain

1. Saint Germain, I am willing to go through "extreme reality therapy" in order to transcend my dramas. I am also willing to be your instrument for helping others experience extreme reality therapy.

Saint Germain, your alchemy,
with violet fire now sets me free.
Saint Germain, I ever grow,
in freedom's overpowering flow.

O Holy Spirit, flow through me,
I am the open door for thee.
O mighty rushing stream of Light,
transcendence is my sacred right.

2. Saint Germain, I am willing to be your instrument for saying to others what they do not want to hear. Even if I get an unpleasant reaction, I am willing to grow in my ability for the ascended masters to use me. I am willing to be free in what I say to other people.

Saint Germain, your mastery,
of violet flame geometry.
Saint Germain, in you I see,
the formulas that set me free.

O Holy Spirit, flow through me,
I am the open door for thee.
O mighty rushing stream of Light,
transcendence is my sacred right.

3. Saint Germain, help me resolve any pain caused by me confronting others. Help me freely express what I have freely received from Above and learn from every experience.

Saint Germain, in Liberty,
I feel the love you have for me.
Saint Germain, I do adore,
the violet flame that makes all more.

O Holy Spirit, flow through me,
I am the open door for thee.
O mighty rushing stream of Light,
transcendence is my sacred right.

4. Saint Germain, help me let the Holy Spirit blow where it listeth through me, and perform the psycho-spiritual surgery that another person needs.

Saint Germain, in unity,
I will transcend duality.
Saint Germain, my self so pure,
your violet chemistry so sure.

**O Holy Spirit, flow through me,
I am the open door for thee.
O mighty rushing stream of Light,
transcendence is my sacred right.**

5. Saint Germain, help me serve to first challenge a person, and when they have started to see what they need to see, help me give them unconditional love.

Saint Germain, reality,
in violet light I am carefree.
Saint Germain, my aura seal,
your violet flame my chakras heal.

**O Holy Spirit, flow through me,
I am the open door for thee.
O mighty rushing stream of Light,
transcendence is my sacred right.**

6. Saint Germain, help me remain non-attached even if people are unpleasant, accusing me of this or that, and trying to pull me into their dramas. Help me be free to remain above their reaction and let it pass right through me.

Saint Germain, your chemistry,
with violet fire set atoms free.
Saint Germain, from lead to gold,
transforming vision I behold.

O Holy Spirit, flow through me,
I am the open door for thee.
O mighty rushing stream of Light,
transcendence is my sacred right.

7. Saint Germain, help me be there with unconditional love and wisdom when a person has become open. Help me be there with unconditional love, for I have no wounds that I need to act out towards other people before I am willing to talk to them again.

Saint Germain, transcendency,
as I am always one with thee.
Saint Germain, from soul I'm free,
I so delight in being me.

O Holy Spirit, flow through me,
I am the open door for thee.
O mighty rushing stream of Light,
transcendence is my sacred right.

8. Saint Germain, help me truly know that freedom is a real option, that freedom is a choice, and that the choice can be made by only one person, namely myself.

Saint Germain, nobility,
the key to sacred alchemy.
Saint Germain, you balance all,
the seven rays upon my call.

**O Holy Spirit, flow through me,
I am the open door for thee.
O mighty rushing stream of Light,
transcendence is my sacred right.**

9. Saint Germain, I am sealed in the unconditional love that is flowing freely through you and through me as unconditional, infinite Freedom!

Saint Germain, your Presence here,
filling up my inner sphere.
Life is now a sacred flow,
God Freedom I on all bestow.

**O Holy Spirit, flow through me,
I am the open door for thee.
O mighty rushing stream of Light,
transcendence is my sacred right.**

Sealing:

In the name of the Divine Mother, I fully accept that the power of these calls is used to set free the Ma-ter light, so it can outpicture the perfect vision of Christ for my own life, for all people and for the planet. In the name I AM THAT I AM, it is done! Amen.

16 | A NEW TYPE OF
SPIRITUAL COMMUNITY

A dictation by Mother Mary.

If you look at the spiritual and religious movements on this planet, you will see that many of them have been destroyed by internal conflicts. Those that have not been destroyed by internal conflicts have, in most cases, not been destroyed because they were taken over by a group of people with such strong egos and opinions that they established a rigid doctrine, a rigid set of rituals and a rigid culture that no one could dare question.

The fate of most spiritual and religious movements on this planet has been either death or rigidity. There is only a very few examples of spiritual movements who have escaped this for any length of time. Certainly, they are there as bright lights shining in the darkness that covers the earth—the darkness that exists only in the minds and energy fields of human beings.

A new type of spiritual movement

Jesus came to set the stage for the emergence of an entirely new spiritual movement that was nothing like the rigid religion whose representatives challenged and eventually killed him. This is a movement where the human ego cannot gain control, cannot play its games, cannot outplay its dramas—for the Holy Spirit flowing through the people will expose it for what it is.

This was the seed also planted by the Buddha in his attempt to create a Sangha that would sustain the onslaught of the demons of Mara, working through the egos of the very members who claim to be the representatives of the Buddha or the students of the Buddha. Even Buddhism was split into many factions, as so often happens when you have the emergence of a power elite. Then comes the emergence of a counter elite, and the struggle between them causes them to go their separate ways, some creating a new offshoot of the old movement, now claiming this is the only right one—whereas the old one still claims to be the only right one.

This, of course, cannot be the true Sangha of the Buddha, for there is something unresolved here. There is an attachment to a particular expression of the Buddha's teachings, as so many Christians display a clear attachment to the teachings of Christ. Many Muslims display an attachment to a particular interpretation of the teachings brought forth through Mohammed, as Shiites, as Sunnis, or whatever shading it might be.

What we see in the spiritual seekers of this age is the potential to bring our quest to fruition. You can bring forth not simply a spiritual movement that sees itself as different from all those other spiritual movements that are rigid and where the ego runs rampant, thinking that you are ego free or you are better. No, we look to you to have the potential to create and to express an entirely new approach to spirituality where you do not allow

yourselves to enter into that state of clearly defining your movement and your culture, feeling this is who we are as opposed to
those outside.

You do not allow the ego to play that game of separation
and superiority. You allow yourselves to be ever open to the
flow from Above, through whomever the Holy Spirit may blow.
You make sure, of course, that you have the discernment of
what is the Holy Spirit, and what is simply someone outplaying their drama, claiming to have the authority of the ascended
masters or the authority of the Holy Spirit in order to get attention—or control.

No community without communication

If you are to be successful in manifesting and maintaining such
a movement, such a culture, you must – if you are willing – consider the teachings we have given in this book. You must come
to the point, spoken of by Saint Germain, of being free to speak
out when there is something that you know is not right, so that
the ego cannot hide, so that the illusions cannot remain in the
dark where no one can see them for what they are.

This does not mean that you all have to be perfect. On the
contrary, it means that all should be free to express themselves
at their present level of consciousness—and to then be lovingly
shown that the way they look at things might have a slight coloring of some belief in their personal database that is not quite the
highest truth, the highest reality, the highest perspective.

This kind of community is precisely what the Buddha established on earth when he was physically present. He created the
Sangha as a sphere set apart where the demons of Mara could
not run rampant. Those who entered that sphere – that sacred
sphere – had an opportunity to see that there is an alternative
to the consciousness of the world—to the Sea of Samsara, the

sea of suffering. Likewise, Jesus established the same circle with his disciples and others that came in closer contact with him— although some of his disciples could not maintain it, but only had it for brief moments and then lapsed back into their old patterns. Surely, you will see the same today where some of you come to a realization, and you actually see your drama. Then you go back and sleep on it, and come back, and now you are right back in the drama as if nothing had happened.

I desire all of you to see that when you come to the point where you are free, then this does not matter. Even if people outplay their dramas, you will simply refuse to play along with it. If you keep doing this and stay out of the drama, people will either be transformed, or they will find somewhere else where people are more receptive to their dramas. After all, if they do not get what they want from you, then why would they keep trying?

They might leave being very negative, projecting upon you that you are unkind, you are unloving, you are not spiritual, you are not this, or you are not that. Again, if you are free, it will not faze you, for you know that you have not been the doer, you have allowed the greater power to stream through you in an attempt – as an expression of God's unconditional love – to awaken those people. You bow to the Law of Free Will that says they have a right to respond in any way they desire.

The trap of materialism

In order to establish a spiritual community, you need to deal with the energies of the mass consciousness. The energy is an expression of the entire culture of materialism – the pleasure cult – and the unwillingness to actually go beyond that content-ment in the materialistic lifestyle that so many people have. This has, throughout the ages, been probably the greatest trap that has kept people from the spiritual path. So many times people have turned to spirituality only when their material lives fell apart. This, of course, is not the pure motivation for seeking an outer spiritual teacher—for you are not ready to hear that teacher, if he has indeed risen to a certain level, such as the Buddha or Christ.

My gratitude and my joyous love to all who read this book. I will, of course, be perfectly willing to work with each of you individually as you make use of the teachings and tools in this book. Be aware that you need to escape the dream of the automatic salvation, of thinking that Mother Mary will somehow come and magically transform you through some act of intercession or some kind of miraculous healing. I can only help you if you are willing to see what you need to see.

As has been explained by Saint Germain many times, you can be so trapped in the pain of your drama that you cannot see it, you cannot hear it when we communicate from the spiritual realm. We seek to help you, to guide you, to go to the physical people – be it therapists or others – who can help you see—even if you think them imperfect, even if you think the science of psychology imperfect. Trust and be open so that if you get inner guidance to see a certain healer or counselor, then you will trust that you are being guided to that person because I can work with that person and use that person regardless of their worldly education. I can use that person to help you see what you cannot see on your own, and what you cannot hear when I tell you directly in your heart.

If I may give you a little tough love, follow the example of those who followed the inner prompting to seek out healers and psychologists. How hard can it be for you to understand that if others have done so, then you are not above it? How hard is that to see, my beloved? Is it really that tough? If others were helped and attained greater freedom, then you can indeed be helped and attain greater freedom. Be willing to make use of all available means and be open that when someone knocks on your door – even though you think he or she might be an ant – that person just might be the guru disguised as an ant. Heed that guru and be willing to partake of what is offered so that you do not reject it—and thus actually reject me in my attempts to set you free.

With that, my beloved, I seal you in the gratitude of my Mother's heart, and I merge myself into the Presence of the Buddha.

17 | KNOW THE DHARMA IN THE MODERN AGE

A dictation by Gautama Buddha.

The Buddha, the Sangha, the Dharma. The Buddha is the center. The Sangha is the sphere set apart where you can come in from the world and connect to the Buddha. The Dharma is not to remain in the Sangha, but to go out in the world and free those who are trapped by the demons of Mara. These are, in many cases, not external demons, but the internal demons of their illusions, their dramas.

When I appeared on the earth 2,500 years ago – give or take a few centuries – I did not have the opportunity that we of the ascended masters have today. I had to give teachings adapted, not only to the planetary level of consciousness, but to the way that people could express and deal with spiritual teachings. Whereby I mean not only language, but their concepts, their world view, their understanding of themselves and the human psyche.

If you read my teachings, you might see that limitation out-pictured. Although you can certainly go beyond the outer words and be guided by the Spirit to see deeper meanings than were expressed in the words, nevertheless, you will see – if you are honest – that there are many things that you routinely speak of today that were not addressed in my teachings. The awareness, the concepts, were not there in the collective consciousness.

I come primarily to give you that sense of co-measurement, of the opportunity you have today, with the Alpha of the teachings of the ascended masters, and the Omega of the teachings brought forth through the worldly sciences and practices of psychology and healing. I dare say that there has not in the recent history of earth – which I count as being very long, give or take a few million years – been a group of people [meaning all spiritual people] who had a greater opportunity to tune in to the Buddha, to attain that freedom that the Buddha Saint Germain expounded upon. You can then go out and fulfill the Dharma of raising those who are trapped behind the veil of Maya by demonstrating that you have pulled back that veil. You have ripped it down and torn it asunder so that it has no reality in your being.

Forget not the Dharma

What shall it profit a man that he gains the whole world and loses the Dharma? What shall it profit a person that you gain some sense of understanding of spiritual teachings and concepts, but you lose the Dharma, the Omega aspect of going out, sharing it with others with the sole intent of setting them free? You go not to raise yourself or get attention or power or control, but to set them free. You are free, and thus you have no other desire than to see them free of whatever holds them back behind that veil of Maya, of illusion, of unreality, of the illusion that although everything is the Buddha nature, you can still somehow be separated from the Buddha. What folly is this? What folly, indeed.

Be willing to be free—to be *me*, for I, too, am free. Why am I free? Because I am awake! I have awakened myself from my own drama. Do not think that the Buddha was born perfect, as they have attempted to portray that picture of me having these other-worldly birth circumstances as they have done to Jesus. I had many past lifetimes on this planet, having sunk just about as far as you can sink, give or take a few degrees.

I too had created my own drama. But something enabled me to respond to the Presence of Sanat Kumara in the earth, and I realized there had to be more. [In a previous age, the collective consciousness of earth had sunk so low that cosmic counsels were contemplating letting the earth self-destruct. A cosmic being, named Sanat Kumara, volunteered to hold the spiritual balance for the earth until someone from earth would be able to do so. His first two students were Gautama Buddha and Lord Maitreya. Gautama Buddha has since risen to the office of Lord of the World and is now holding the spiritual balance for all life on earth.]

I started that journey, pulling back the veils of illusion that made up my drama. I came to the point where I could sit under the Bo tree and face the demons of Mara, which were – at least in the first initiation – not the demons of the world, but the demons of my own past dramas seeking to pull me back into them. I would not be pulled hither or yon, for I had awakened and could see through every one of the dramas and the illusions that created them. I remained free in that awakeness, that Flame of Awakeness that I am.

There is no real separation

The Buddha nature is awake and aware that it is everything, and that there is nothing outside of it—thus seeing the Buddha nature in any manifestation in the world of form, no matter how temporary and unreal it might be. Even the concept of a veil of Maya has the danger of making you think that there is some real separation between Maya and the Sangha of the Buddha. Even the concept of a path makes you think that you really are separated. You have to go though this long and arduous process of entering the Sangha or the kingdom of God, or whatever it may be that you long for.

There is no actual separation. The only thing that separates you from the kingdom of God and from the Sangha of the Buddha is your own drama. There is no objective force that separates you. I am not saying there are not other self-aware beings – or even the demons who are not actually self-aware anymore – who are external to you. But they can only influence you through your own subjective reality of giving them power. As I explained last year at New Year's time, that evil lord sitting at the temple at the top of the mountain simply is not there and was never there. The illusion of his existence has been kept alive only by the people who have chosen to create a drama that necessitated that ultimate evil, and thus feeding it their energy. [Refers to a dictation by Gautama Buddha in which he described an imaginary temple that supposedly housed the ultimate evil being, controlling a hierarchy of evildoers. No one had ever entered the temple, and in reality it was empty, meaning that all those who work against Oneness are driven by an illusion.]

Let it all collapse like a house of cards. Let it all collapse. Just let it go, my beloved, and enter the Sangha. How do you enter the Sangha? Well, through the door, of course. Where is the door? Where is it, my beloved? [Audience answers, "Within us"] In your hearts, in your hearts.

Look beyond normal communication

In the process of learning more about communicating from the heart, you have also learned hidden keys to communicating with the heart—thus entering the heart. The common concept of communication on earth is that you need to communicate because there is a distance between you and another. Communication is a way to cross the distance, and it is so, to some degree. There are higher degrees of understanding, and the highest form of communication is actually communion, leading to union, meaning oneness.

You may think I am a distant Being, communicating with you through a messenger who is external to yourself. So it is, because your current drama has created the illusion that you are separated from me—and thus you need some external means of communication. I do not see myself as separated from you. You are perfectly capable of communicating with me inside your own heart.

How do you communicate with me? By coming into communion with me, by being willing to move towards oneness with the Buddha. How do you become a messenger who can speak for the Buddha—let the Buddha speak through him? By being willing to come into oneness because you are not afraid to let all that is anti-buddha be exposed so that you can see its unreality, give it up and just let it fade away. Each and every one of you have that ability to come into oneness with me, and thus become an open door for – in some measure, as it is individually mandated in your divine plans – serving to bring forth the true teachings of the Christ and the Buddha and all other spiritual teachers.

Reaching out to people from any tradition

The culture, the movement, that Mother Mary talked about is certainly one that transcends all outer barriers and divisions. It has the potential to reach out to people from any spiritual tradition – or no spiritual tradition – by speaking that universal language of the heart. You have become so free that when you meet any person, you are free to let the Spirit speak to them in the language that they can understand and that has the biggest opportunity to open up their hearts.

They can have a glimpse that there is something beyond the veil of Maya—something beyond the drama that they have so far thought was so real. They see in you that you are free, at peace, happy, joyful—and you are not in their drama. They see that there is an alternative. You can indeed be fulfilled without the drama—but by simply *being, being, being* without playing a role that is not you, that you have only taken on and thus forgotten your inner being.

Sense the intensity of my peace that is immovable. Do you sense it, my beloved? Do you sense that I am not caught up in your personal drama? When you go out in the world and, once again, are tempted to fall back into that drama – or perhaps, fall back into it but then suddenly wake up and realize you slipped – then think back to this sense that I, the Buddha, am not in your drama. I am everywhere! If you will but attune your awareness to me, you can reconnect to that sense that there is indeed a reality outside your drama.

This is – really – the simplest way to explain the spiritual path and the role of a spiritual teacher: to serve as that point of reality outside the student's personal drama. The person can gradually separate itself from the drama and be free as the teacher is free. Be sealed then, in that peace that I AM. For when you are awake, how can you not be at peace?

About the Author

Kim Michaels is an accomplished writer and author. He has conducted spiritual conferences and workshops in 14 countries, has counseled hundreds of spiritual students and has done numerous radio shows on spiritual topics. Kim has been on the spiritual path since 1976. He has studied a wide variety of spiritual teachings and practiced many techniques for raising consciousness. Since 2002 he has served as a messenger for Jesus and other ascended masters. He has brought forth extensive teachings about the mystical path, many of them available for free on his websites: *www.askrealjesus.com*, *www.ascendedmasteranswers.com*, *www.ascendedmasterlight.com* and *www.transcendencetoolbox.com*. For personal information, visit Kim at *www.KimMichaels.info*.

Flowing with the River of Life Exercise Book

This book is the companion to "Flowing With the River of Life" and contains four unique invocations based on the teachings by the Maha Chohan. The invocations are designed to help you accomplish the following:

- Rise above the death consciousness,
- Attain freedom from aggressive spirits seeking to influence you,
- Expose the spirit in your own being that is holding you back right now,
- Help you let go of spirits in your own being.

This book also contains abbreviated teachings on the death consciousness and how you create and transcend spirits.

Part two of the book contains all of the decrees you use in the seven-month vigil to the spiritual rays. This vigil is designed to help you become familiar with the creative energies of the seven rays and thus unlock your creative potential. You will also find short descriptions of the pure qualities and the perversions of each ray.

The Song of Life Healing Matrix

Every day we experience situations where we are exposed to uncertainties, mental or emotional disturbances, positive or negative stress. Everything we go through leaves a mark on our personal story. Some are uplifting positive memories, others are painful to a degree that we suppress them in order to escape the trauma. Each detail of our personal story reveals part of who we are and what blocks our growth. In these spheres of our personal stories we hide our deepest beliefs, concepts, feelings and thoughts that all affect the way we look at life, each other and ourselves. This often generates diseases in our mental, emotional or physical bodies.

The Song of Life Healing Matrix provides you with the unique tools to bring to light the deepest details of your of own song of life. This highly effective tool contains the teachings from eight representatives of the Divine Mother—the ascended masters who represent the Divine Feminine for planet earth. They address the blocks to your personal healing and introduce a highly effective tool for sound healing in the form of the Song Life. The eight invocations that you can easily learn, allow you to call forth the following types of healing:

- The transformation of your sense of identity so you realize you are a spiritual being in a human body.

- The clearing of your mental body from all blocking illusions and destructive thought patterns.
- The healing of emotional wounds and the release of the accumulated negative feelings that reinforce self-destructive reactionary patterns.
- The healing of the organs and systems in your physical body from any disease.
- The healing of all lack of balance that prevents you from manifesting your goals in life.
- The healing of all sense of lack that block the manifestation of a spiritually and materially abundant life.
- The healing of all blocks to your acceptance of unconditional love and the flow of love through your being.
- The healing of the denial of your true identity as a co-creator with God and the fact that we are all are part of the Divine Feminine.

CPSIA information can be obtained at www.ICGtesting.com
Printed in the USA
BVOW08s0332300116

434812BV00002B/18/P